Julian Opie

Julian Opie

Lynne Cooke
Wulf Herzogenrath
Ulrich Loock
Michael Newman
James Roberts

Thames and Hudson

Contents

A selection of drawings, and photographs taken by the artist, run alongside the texts

Foreword

A number of strikingly original sculptors based in this country have emerged on the international scene in the past decade. The Hayward Gallery has played its part in defining and encouraging this phenomenon, both through group exhibitions – from The Sculpture Show in 1983 to The British Art Show of 1990 – and through presentations of work by individual artists, including Tony Cragg in 1987 and Richard Long in 1991. The nature of the Hayward's spaces, in themselves distinctly sculptural, has encouraged presentations of three-dimensional work.

Julian Opie's presence here with a major individual exhibition should not come as a surprise. However, it does signal a development in the South Bank Centre's exhibitions policy at the Hayward. As an expression of faith in an artist still relatively young, it marks our desire to place the work of contemporary artists in the foreground of our programme, and to provide the space and facilities which will enable the work to achieve its full impact. Opie has been an influential figure on the British art scene ever since his emergence in the early 1980s, and he first attracted international attention in 1984 through his startling contribution to documenta 8 in Kassel. Moving from the prodigiously inventive painted metal sculptures of the early 1980s, Opie worked his way through a dizzying range of new ideas, materials and conceits before going on to produce clearly defined bodies of work, highly consistent within themselves but outwardly quite distinct from one another. All these developments are represented in the current exhibition, though we have placed the emphasis on work made within the past year, culminating in a return to imagistic painting within a sculptural context. Three features unite this work: a restless enquiry into the nature of sculptural form, a deftness of fabrication, and the many points of contact afforded with the world 'outside' sculpture – notably, the fabricated worlds of architecture, design and technology.

We are above all grateful to Julian Opie himself for the enthusiasm with which he has taken up our invitation and the thought he has put into every aspect of this project. We are also much indebted to the Lisson Gallery, and in particular to Nicholas Logsdail, Sharon Essor, Susan Waxman, Jo Spark and Emma Sandbach, for their constant encouragement and practical advice and support. Many others, too, have contributed to the realisation of the exhibition and catalogue. We thank Wulf Herzogenrath, Ulrich Loock, James Roberts, Lynne Cooke and Michael Newman, who have all been engaged with Opie's work at various points, and have contributed important texts to the catalogue; and Herman Lelie, who has designed the catalogue in close collaboration with the artist. We are delighted that the exhibition is to travel to the Kunstverein Hannover after its London showing, and thank the Director, Eckhard Schneider, for his enthusiastic support of the project. We are grateful to The Henry Moore Foundation for support of the catalogue, and to Belle Shenkman and British Alcan Aluminium PLC for their support in kind. We are also grateful to Qumar Islam of Maxtrans, London, Allan Halliday of Travis Perkins and Clifford Rankin of Rankin's Glass for their support. Finally, I should like to express warm thanks to my colleague, Martin Caiger-Smith, who has worked closely with the artist in seeing this exciting project through, from its inception to its successful realisation.

Henry Meyric Hughes
Director of Exhibitions

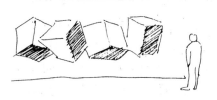

Front cover of the catalogue for the 1984 Julian Opie exhibition at the Kölnischer Kunstverein

Julian Opie: an introduction

Wulf Herzogenrath

Before you is an object. On its front is a strong, black oval on a yellow field, with some areas heightened in white, others loosely painted brown, like areas of shadow. On the reverse is a white rectangle on a red ground, again with highlights and shadows. Only by picking the object up and looking at its edge do you see that it is a catalogue, with the words 'Julian Opie, Kölnischer Kunstverein' printed on the spine. This was the catalogue of the 1984 Cologne exhibition.

This coloured object deliberately plays on the idea of being a book. The painterly gestures, which appear out of proportion to the book, suggest that this must be an original object, even if you cannot immediately recognise the material that it is made of. Flicking through the pages, you realise that its covers are of thin card. The artist conjures notions of a painting, an object and a book in such a way that all three apparently distinct elements coalesce into an original multiple, which serves the function of a catalogue or book, just as it acts as an illustration of one.

I have gone into such detail because this catalogue offers a perfect illustration of the artistic intentions behind Julian Opie's painted metal objects of the first half of the 1980s: they were unpretentious and playful, yet deliberately undermined the conventional distinctions between painting, sculpture and fabricated objects. In a text he wrote for his Tate Gallery exhibition in July 1983, Opie stated: 'I don't really paint or sculpt, but draw. I use any material that seems appropriate or easy to do the drawings.' In other words, he likens the metal wall reliefs, with their bright, colourful appearance, to 'drawings', executed in a loose, relaxed style.

While on a visit to London in February 1984, as a guest of the British Council, I went to Julian Opie's studio, in the company of Nicholas Logsdail, of the Lisson

Gallery, and Jennifer Brügelmann, a keen collector of contemporary art from Cologne. Opie had just moved into a house in Hampstead, and the household furnishings mingled freely with his richly suggestive, colourful objects. Suspended from a hand-wrought metal standard-lamp was a sequence of painted metal letters spelling the word LONELY, shaped out of metal and illuminated by the lamp itself. This motif was reminiscent of René Magritte, but it had been re-appropriated and given a private meaning, tinged with irony. A work entitled *Four Parking Tickets* showed a large yellow number four, framed by four car windscreen wipers, which were clamping down parking tickets. In contrast, the number Five was surrounded by five paintings, rough copies of a Frans Hals, a Manet, a van Gogh, a Picasso and a Mondrian – all hand-painted onto metal surfaces. A number of paintings, including some of the aforementioned, re-done in a practical, almost square format, appeared to spill out of a suitcase with the aptly punning title *Cultural Baggage*. In another work, *A Pile of Old Masters* (supposedly authentic masterpieces) lie around in the corner, like cheap copies. Perhaps Opie was referring to the burden placed on the young artist who tries to deal creatively with the weight of art history?

As a long-time admirer of Richard Long's intense, single-minded endeavours and of Ian Hamilton Finlay's strangely compelling sculptures, I sensed that I was witnessing something entirely new to contemporary British sculpture, which I had previously always linked with nature and the landscape. Here was a young artist engaging in a single-minded discourse about art and its meanings, through his use of quite different media, methods and wit, to produce urban sculptures which drew on the artistic traditions of the city. Along with the work of his rather older peers, Tony Cragg and Bill Woodrow, I took this to signal a revitalisation of the somewhat tired tradition of sculpture in stone and metal, through the use of everyday materials, simple working methods, themes from everyday life, ironic or anarchic attitudes, and a deliberately critical stance towards the intellectual arguments which dominated the artistic debates of the day.

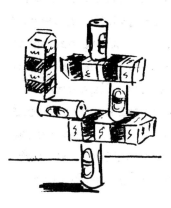

I had remained somewhat unconvinced by the attempts of many artists in Germany to create a new kind of sculpture by carving direct into the wood with anything from an axe to conventional hand tools, and painting the broad exposed surfaces: this seemed to me too close to expressionist antecedents of the 1910s and '20s. So where was one to look for a new approach to sculpture? It struck me that here, in this British work, was a new spirit of irreverence, which might enrich the artistic debate in Cologne, at a time when the painters of the Mülheimer Freiheit, Dokoupil, Dahn, Adamski, Bömmels and others were enlivening the scene with their cheekily refreshing paintings, actions and concerts, and the group associated with the music magazine *Spex* were establishing links between the avant-garde and the pop music of the moment.

In retrospect, Opie's works in those years of the mid 80s had an important effect on his development. Their loose style and playful inquisitiveness helped him to develop a language of much greater discipline and formal consistency, which took him beyond the imaginative and diverse ideas of his early sketchbooks. Opie's home, when I saw it in 1984, looked not unlike many of his works: he had piled up the books which had fallen off their shelves in much the same way as he had represented them in his sculpture. One small work of his impressed me in particular: a thick book on art history, the pages of which appeared to be blown about by the wind and flying away – what a perfect start for a young artist aiming to surpass the wisdom of his forebears, as if by counting up to five he could conjure up all the available classics and banish them, at a stroke!

One of Opie's working principles, which had fascinated me, on reflection, was that the sculptures all had two sides – a front, treated in a painterly manner, and a back which was simply left flat, metallic and unadorned, so that any trace of illusion was dispelled by the sight of the tin sheet of which the sculpture was composed. This made it clear, once and for all, that the paint was intentionally applied so loosely and spontaneously that Opie could never have intended a *trompe*

l'oeil effect. As I wrote at the time, in my introduction to the catalogue: 'His aim is not to create a false reality, through imitation, but to develop an artistic medium for the formation of a visual language.' This visual language was designed to establish a connection between literature (letters, words, books), painting (colour and form) and sculpture (three-dimensional and relief).

In Cologne in 1984, Julian Opie drew his name in my visitors' book in 'sculpted' yellow letters, running down a wall as if in relief: his 'J, U, L, I, A, N' was flanked by the palette of a great painter of the traditional kind and the paint bucket of a modern, all-round artist. Interspersed between these were a stretcher, a portfolio and a book, both descriptive and evocative of their particular worlds. Painting thus became the embodiment of the sculptor's longing and yet issued an ironic challenge to the absurdity of artistic hierarchies. Did not all art contrast with the stuff of real life (the bread and wine drawn around his surname, O, P, I, E, below) by transposing reality onto a higher plane, at the risk, perhaps, of falling flat on its face? The last colour reproduction in the Cologne catalogue shows an image of four letters F, U, C, K, with the C facing the wrong way. The title, *Experiment in Volume*, leaves the spectator unsure of the nature of the experiment involved: word and meaning, relief and painting, depth and humour – all from a young artist on the way to putting together a consistent and ever more clearly contoured body of work, which introduced a chilling logic into his sculpture, on the heels of his warming wit.

The exhibition referred to above was held from 16 August to 28 October 1984 at the Cologne Kunstverein, with the support of Anneliese Greulich of the British Council. It was presented alongside four new, large sculptures by Tony Cragg. One of the most agreeable consequences of the exhibition, still to be seen today, was the sculpture commissioned from Julian Opie by Walter König, a committee member of the Kunstverein. This consisted of a large wall-piece depicting a cascade of falling books on the façade of the König bookshop – one of the most important meeting places for artists in Cologne – on the corner of the Ehrenstrasse and Albertusstrasse.

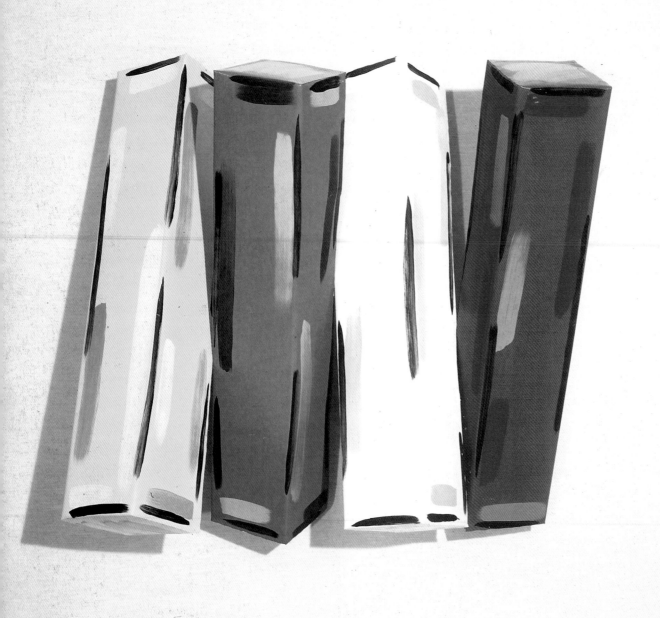

About £40 Worth of Steel
1984, oil paint on steel
150 × 180 × 75 cm

A Pile of Old Masters
1983, oil paint on steel
37 × 37 × 6 cm each (14 parts)

Incident in the Library II
1983, oil paint on steel
165 × 100 × 30 cm

A to B
1984, oil paint on steel
50 × 150 × 10 cm

This One Took Ages to Make
1983, oil paint on steel
height 120 cm

Legend of Europa
1984, oil paint on steel
170 × 100 × 60 cm

Project for Heathrow
1985, oil paint on steel
45 × 140 × 60 cm

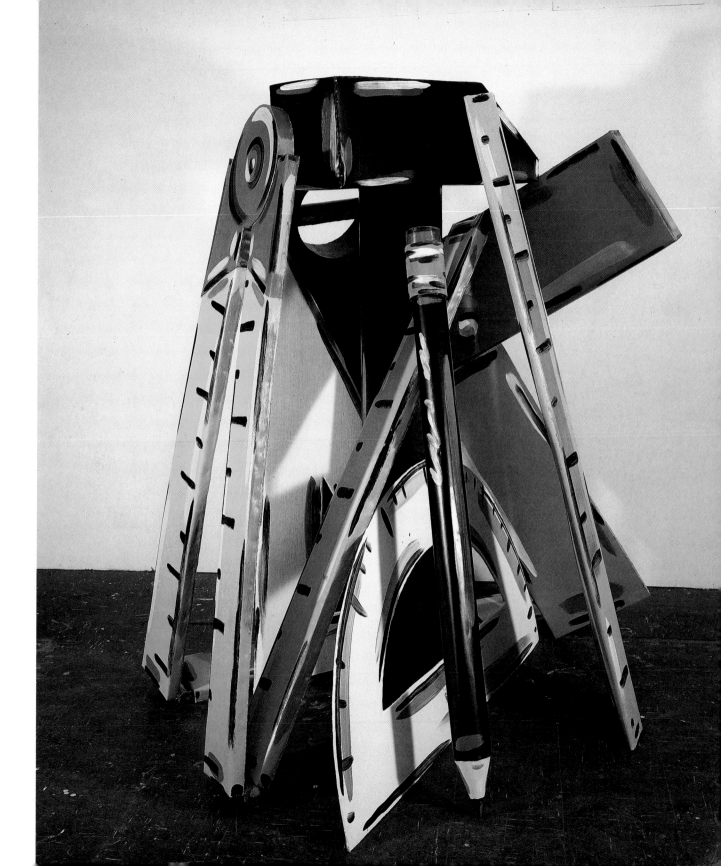

Broken Rules
1985, oil paint on steel
213 × 152 × 183 cm

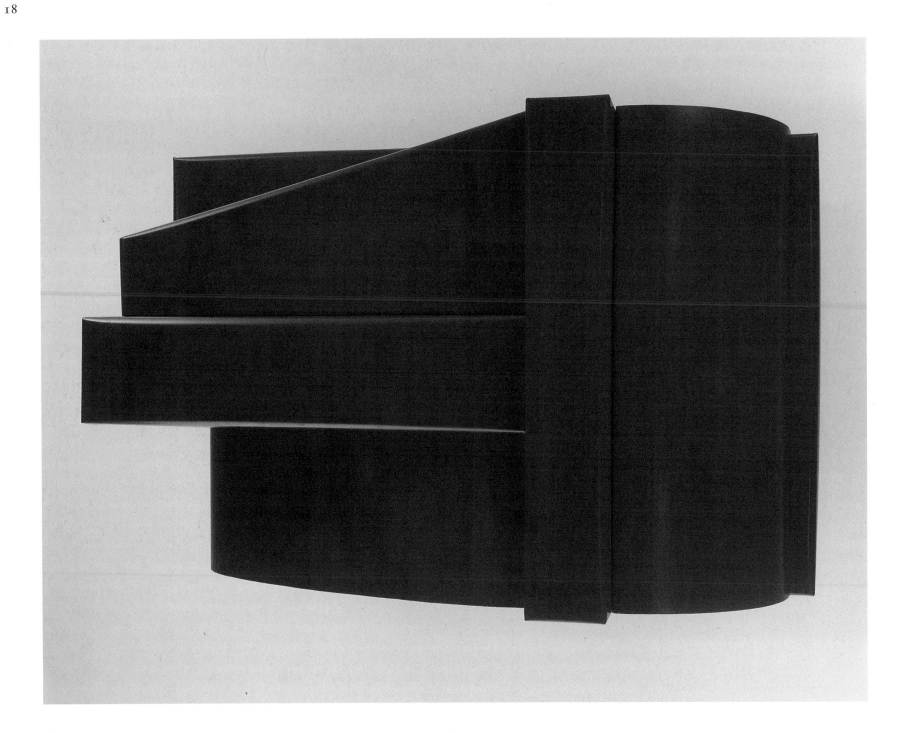

Spies
1986, cellulose paint on steel
90 × 90 × 105 cm

Ceasefire
1986, cellulose paint on steel
90 × 90 × 175 cm

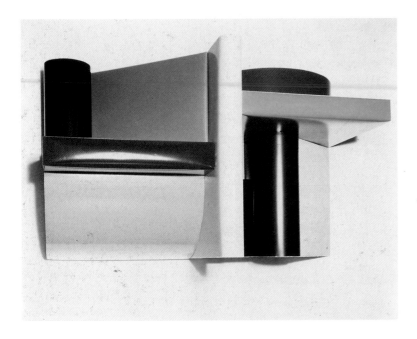

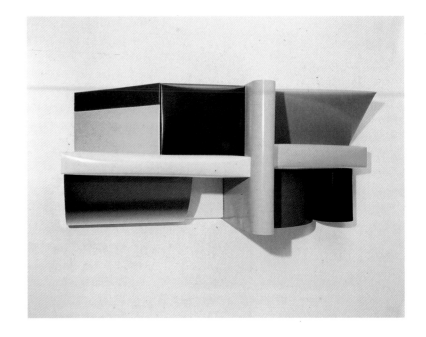

Divided They Stand, Divided They Fall
1986, cellulose paint on steel
125 × 215 × 90 cm

Man Accused of Murder (11 colours)
1986, cellulose paint on steel
200 × 100 × 96 cm

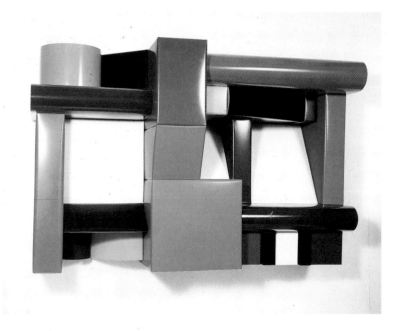

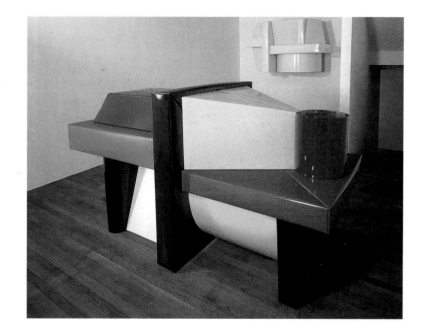

Postal Staff Return to Work
1986, cellulose paint on steel
250 × 150 × 65 cm

Cruise
1986, cellulose paint on steel
100 × 110 × 220 cm

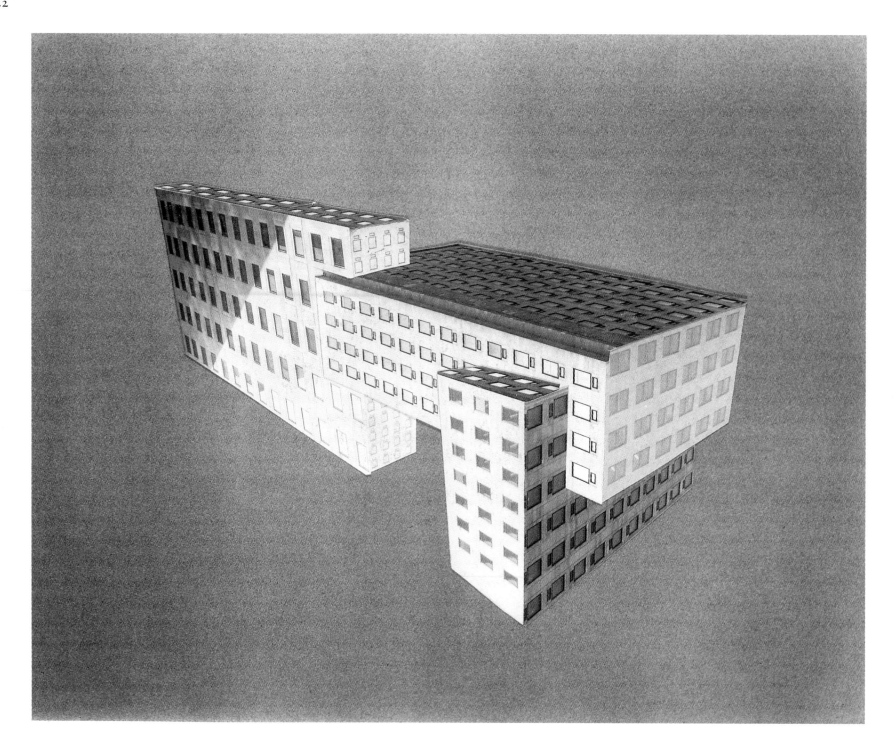

Untitled
1987, photo collage
20.5 × 29.5 cm

Untitled
1987, photo collage
20.5 × 29.5 cm

M.
1988, 2 parts, aluminium, stainless steel,
foam, PVC, wood, cellulose paint
32 × 55.5 × 18.5 cm each

H.
1987, aluminium, stainless steel,
foam, PVC, wood, cellulose paint
130.5 × 218 × 28 cm

J.
1987, glass, aluminium, stainless steel,
foam, PVC, wood
127 × 217 × 27 cm

G.
1987, glass, aluminium, stainless steel,
foam, PVC, wood, cellulose paint
63.5 × 181 × 86 cm

n.,o.
1988, 2 parts, plastic, aluminium,
wood, rubber, cellulose paint
172 × 62 × 66 cm

131 × 173 × 9
1989, aluminium, glass, plastic,
wood, rubber, cellulose paint
131 × 173 × 9 cm

Night Light, (16/2222CC)
(back view)
1989, rubber, aluminium, glass,
plastic, wood, stainless steel,
fluorescent light
186 × 124 × 40 cm

Night Light, (19/1343GY)
(back view)
1989, rubber, aluminium, glass,
plastic, wood, stainless steel,
fluorescent light
187 × 123 × 45 cm

Night Light, (17/1222GY)
(back view)
1989, rubber, aluminium, glass,
plastic, wood, stainless steel,
fluorescent light
188 × 125 × 42 cm

(12/3343BB)
(back view)
1989, rubber, aluminium, glass,
plastic, wood, fluorescent light,
rubber, cellulose paint
186 × 127 × 38 cm

Night Light (26/5444CY)
(back view)
1989, rubber, anodised
aluminium, glass, wood, zincoid,
fluorescent light
186 × 124 × 40 cm

Night Light (24/1343BY)
(back view)
1989, rubber, aluminium, glass,
wood, galvanised steel, cellulose
paint, fluorescent light
186 × 124 × 40 cm

Night Light (22/3333CY)
(back view)
1989, rubber, aluminium, glass,
plastic, wood, cellulose paint,
fluorescent light
186 × 124 × 43 cm

Night Light (25/333CB)
(back view)
1989, rubber, aluminium, glass,
plastic, wood, cellulose paint,
fluorescent light
186 × 124 × 42 cm

Night Light (24/1343BY)
1989, wood, glass, rubber,
aluminium, cellulose paint,
fluorescent light, galvanised steel
186 × 124 × 40 cm

Overleaf:
Installation, OBJECTives,
The New Sculpture, Newport
Harbor Museum, 1990

Beyond the architectural

Ulrich Loock

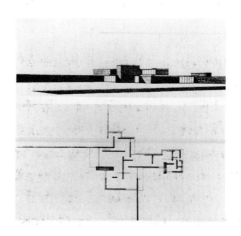

Mies van der Rohe
Brick Country House, 1923

Mies van der Rohe
Hubbe House, Perspective view of court, 1935
pencil drawing on board
48.3 × 67.3 cm

The works which Julian Opie produced around 1990 – his *Houses*, *Shelf Units* and *Columns* – are most interesting, perhaps, for their reference to the notion of a transition from art to architecture. This is a notion central to modernism itself, and in touching on it Opie focuses on a paradigmatic and well-defined moment in modernism's history, adopting his own, contemporary position within, or rather in the light of, that moment – evoking, and at the same time deconstructing, this paradigm. This stance, I would argue, allows Opie to address another, newer transition (be it under way, impending or merely imagined) from the rational reconstruction of reality – that shibboleth of modernism – to the virtuality of reality. The two share, if nothing else, at least an aspiration to totality. (Here I am thinking, of course, of a much broader phenomenon than those technical gadgets such as gloves and helmets which transport you into a world of 'virtual reality', or than the effect of computer imaging on architecture.) Opie's works of around this time seem to make use of 'obsolete' media – that is, the sculptural or architectural presence of an 'object' – in order to address the problems which are widely thought of as intrinsically linked to the reign of the most advanced – electronic – media.

Since the beginning of this century, it is true, painting and sculpture have taken architecture as a vanishing point – perhaps, even, the most important one. Not all the diverse avant-gardes of this century have subscribed to this view, however. Ideas of architecture as the *mater artium* received new impetus in the '70s and '80s, but only in the context of a conservative, anti-modernist impulse, which, like so many other ideas, has been attributed to 'post-modernism'. The relationship of the historical avant-gardes to architecture also diverged from the conception of a

dialectical relationship between art works and given architectural conditions – Richard Serra's site-specific sculptures, for example, or even the interventions of Michael Asher, which refer to the paradigm of sculpture, even if they do so only to relinquish all sculptural autonomy and identify, or unmask, criticise and elude the institutional – and hence architectural – conditions and presuppositions of the constitution of the work of art.

Early this century, following on from his suprematist paintings, Malevich constructed his 'Architectonic' models, El Lissitzky called his *Proun* works 'transit stops for architecture', Piet Mondrian said that his own painting would be superfluous once the world (and not just the architectural world) was recast according to the principles manifested in his works. Such attitudes posit a *transition* from visual art, fundamentally autonomous painting or sculpture, to the overall functionalism of architecture. They anticipate the general reconstruction of the environment at the cost of the individual artistic, or even architectural, object. This, among other things, is what we nowadays refer to as the utopia of modernism.

Architects closely connected with artists, such as those of De Stijl or the Bauhaus, the Russian Constructivists and Le Corbusier in particular, began to conceive and build what must be considered truly modern architecture. They showed a common refusal to close off the interior of the building from the outside, since the architectural construction was seen as one formal element within the overall spatial continuum. One interesting design in this respect was by the young Mies van der Rohe, who, in his *Brick Country House* of 1922, for instance, proposed that certain walls run far beyond the contained boundaries of the house, so as to structure architecturally the surrounding grounds as well as the house itself.

Obviously, this way of thinking about architecture places the utmost importance on transparency: the American architect Philip Johnson, for example, taking his lead from Mies van der Rohe, built the famous *Glass House* in New Canaan,

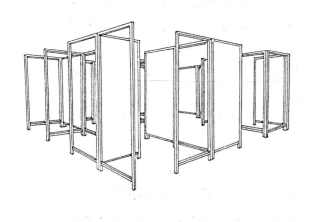

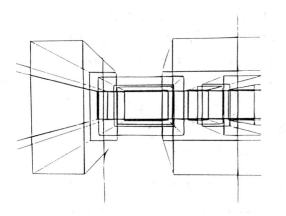

Connecticut, in 1949, the entire outer shell of which is transparent. As for the notion of the eclipse of the architectural object, which Mies upheld until quite late in his career – though only for very particular projects such as the National Gallery in Berlin (1962–68) – it is interesting to take a look at his own early 'utopian' architectural drawings. In these, architectural structures appear, to a large extent, dissolved. It is as though they merge with the white of the paper, modulating it; the drawings are immediately clear analogies for the integration of urban architecture. But the human figures in these drawings are black, and heavily drawn, set apart from the seamless transition between the architecture and its surroundings. They look like 'punctuations' of the design represented; they exist as breaks in the continuum of space. They remain outside transparency's claim to universality, because it is *for* and *out of* the human figure that transparency is organised. These particular drawings by Mies reveal the humanistic origins and humanistic definition of the modern conception of architecture. Of course, transparency in architecture relates directly to more general rationalist notions of the transparency of all social relations, and resistance to mythical obfuscation.

As we know, glass architecture, developed during the '20s, became enormously popular after World War Two, from panoramic vistas to display windows, to the glass façades of administrative buildings. The effect is obvious: the glass panels imply unlimited visual access, either distracting attention from the fact that access is actually denied – as privacy is nevertheless preserved, opacity and inaccessibility of (economic) power persists – or intensifying the desire on the part of the viewer to buy whatever is on display. Many works by the American artist Dan Graham, particularly those in which he works with sheets of glass, semi-transparent glass, mirrors, two-way mirrors, video and delayed playback, can be read as investigations into the asymmetry of real relations, as communicated by transparency and reflection: I can/cannot see you, whilst you can/cannot see me; whilst I see myself/you (in the mirror/on the video screen), I no longer see

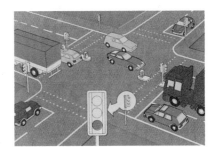

myself/you ... With his experimental arrangements, and even more with his architectural projects like *Alteration to a suburban house* of 1978, Dan Graham embarks on a sustained contradiction of the modern myth of transparency, playing, in many different ways, with the connection between accessibility and denial, and illuminating it in metaphorical form – illuminating it for a 'user' of the visual machine, who is exposed to it and serves it in equal measure, but who is finally expected to reflect on what happens to him there, thus being granted an insight into the ideological functions of transparency and related means of representation in architecture and elsewhere.

Opie's works, then, of 1990, the *Houses*, *Shelf Units* and *Columns*, seem to pick up on the avant-garde's expectation of a transition from visual art to architecture. His 'labyrinth' *Constructions* of 1989 seem 'transitional' works, more akin to those earlier pieces that had preoccupied him for some considerable time, which allude to everyday objects such as freezers, air-conditioning systems or showcases. The 'labyrinths' exist so that the visitor can enter their sphere and move through them, undergoing a specific physical and spatial experience that contrasts with our everyday experience of space – a new and different experience based principally on visual insecurity, since spatial openings and the transparency or semi-transparency of glass walls, various mirroring effects and repeated modular elements block any immediate or clear orientation in space. In these works Opie refers to elements of modernist transparent architecture: the design of airports, exhibition centres or shopping malls springs to mind. But I call the 'labyrinths' transitional works because they are dominated by the effect of simulation that characterises the object-related pieces, whilst on the other hand there is as yet no convincing definition of their architectural dimension. They have too much of the character of environments or installations to fully induce the experience of the self and the body.

In the *Houses*, however, Opie confronts the problem of the transition from visual art or sculpture to architecture. It is, for example, far from clear how the *Houses*

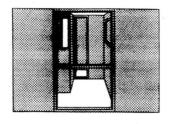

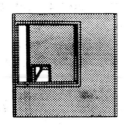

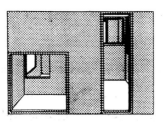

should be categorised. They have the scale of sculpture and share certain of its characteristics, not least in their clear, cubic external form and uniform white colour; they might be linked with the principles of minimal art, although it would be difficult to find direct models for them; and they might reproduce particular architectural elements: the foreman's hut on a factory shop floor, the office portacabin on a building-site. But they can also be seen as architectural models, and thus they clearly refer to modern architecture such as that of De Stijl – the very architecture that attempted to dissolve the architectural object.

It is impossible to enter these works; they are accessible only to the eye, and indeed several large windows ensure that there is plenty of visual access. The physical inaccessibility of these works is not incidental: it is one of their main distinguishing features. This means that man, as viewer or occupier, is not at the centre of the works – as, for example, in Mies's architectural drawings, or even in Dan Graham's installations. We are excluded. The sculptural and architectural construction lacks that central referent from which it takes its bearings and derives its form. Void of this centre, each of Opie's *Houses* is left to itself; that is what is presented.

What is presented is a construct that displays the integration of inner and outer in exemplary fashion, through the medium of transparency. This can perhaps be seen most clearly in the fact that the *Houses* are open at the bottom (and the top) and that a glance inside reveals, running through them, the floor of wherever they are sited. The outer walls alternate solid surfaces and panes of glass, and other interior wall surfaces fitted with windows obstruct the eye. Certain parts of the inner space remain hidden from view. From some angle, some particular viewpoint, however, each and every hidden corner can be seen, yet no significantly new visual experience is supplied; the information to be gleaned about the work's internal structure is not substantively increased. For everything that is on view, it might still be said that there is nothing to be seen – despite the visual access granted by transparency. In

Opie's *Houses* transparency itself becomes the subject – but the transparency of transparency is, in a sense, only a form of opacity. Thrown back upon itself, comprehensive transparency in the *Houses* is constructed as the opposite of the avant-garde conception of transparency. It seems appropriate to introduce the idea of deconstruction in regard to this process. The deconstruction of modernist transparency in Opie's *Houses* differs significantly from the illumination of the ideological implications of the concept of transparency in Graham's installations. Opie's works strip transparency of its ideological power by removing the object from the medium of communication; this results in a closed circuit.

The exclusion of external reference, however, means that the *Houses* cease to be 'reliable', definite and finite objects. It is entirely appropriate that Opie should have built not only two different, and yet identically constructed, *Houses*, but that he has also exhibited them side by side (as, for example, in the Kunsthalle in Berne in 1991). There could have been even more, and that would have produced more and more different possible views of the interior, without allowing any qualitative change.

I have emphasised the exclusion of the viewer, the user, from works such as Opie's *Houses* and *Boxes*. It is true that we are positioned, and held, outside the works; and yet seeing them, looking at or through them we are at the same time connected with them. This notion of being connected to the object we behold seems appropriate in many ways, not least for its connotation of electronic imaging. It must be clearly distinguished from the notion of perception in the phenomenological sense, in which perception is taken as the visual recreation of an object. In relation to Opie's *Houses* or *Boxes*, seeing is either a matter of looking at or looking through; the only choice left to us, the viewer, is whether to open or close our eyes. Being visually connected to one of these works means to be controlled by its premises, which are organised in a yes/no, or 0:1 manner – like the channels of digitalised information. So here Opie is appropriating the mode of

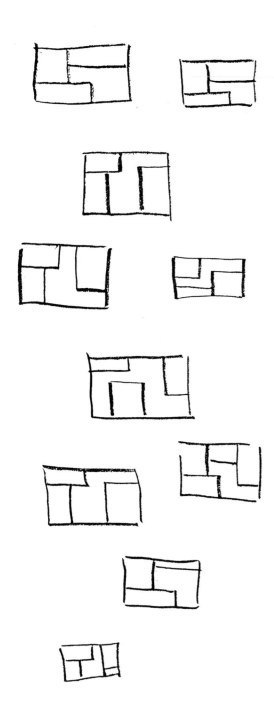

computer processing, and in doing so he is placing what we would previously have taken to be the viewer, or user, in the position of the subject within electronically produced – or virtual – reality.

What is so interesting is that Opie, in his deconstruction of modernist transparency, is using these working methods of electronic image-production in a three-dimensional, physical and haptic medium – using them 'against the grain'. Works of this kind suggest a further consideration of views postulating a progressive development of the (artistic) means of production, which would render older art-forms obsolete. We might consider, on the other hand, whether the 'older' media are not particularly well suited to furthering our understanding of developments which, in the newest media, remain in many ways incomprehensible.

Translated by Shaun Whiteside

Spam for Tea

James Roberts

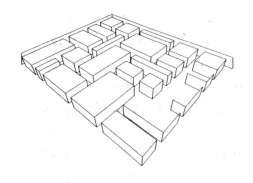

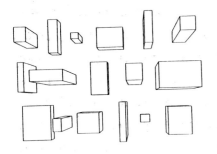

Somewhere inside a computer near you is a large city. Laid out in a modernist grid, its street plan is regular, yet not without variation, and through its networks of roads and corridors electrons run like rush-hour commuters on speed, stopping impatiently at certain junctions and flowing en masse across others. There is no aimless loitering and there is no jay walking. This systematic modern city is a micro-architecture whose operation, essentially comprising the crossing and not-crossing of junctions, performs simple logical functions: it decides whether things are the same, different, greater or smaller, and adds them together. This world, hidden during the performance of routine computerised tasks such as word-processing and spreadsheet analysis, comes to the surface in computer games. Early games such as *Pac-Man*, conceived and executed for the most part by programmers, literally replicated the functions and often the formal arrangement of this city on a larger, but simplified, level. These were binary games in which the paths to be negotiated were either open or closed and the limitations of movement and action were strictly defined. Life was simple then: you could either go or you couldn't and there were few decisions to be made. As microchip architecture has developed in speed and complexity, the worlds described in computer games have reached a correspondingly greater degree of sophistication. Perhaps now you can travel faster in your journey, the obstacles you approach may appear to be different from one another and the scenery surrounding the active area of the game may appear three-dimensional, nicely modelled and rendered; but essentially there is no difference – if you are at certain co-ordinates at a certain time, you die. The limitations of worlds conceived to run on microprocessors raise some interesting questions: are these limitations inherent in the system design, forcing the creation of

worlds that embrace these restrictions to work fully within them, or is the architecture itself merely symptomatic of the failure of classical mathematical and logical rules to describe adequately the world of experience through which we move in everyday life?

From the point of view of an unimaginative architect, town planner, or government, it would be ideal if people actually did perform only a limited and strictly defined set of functions. Housing problems, health care, agricultural production and energy supply could be controlled to a degree where they became an exact science with not one statistical blip on the horizon. In a certain sense, this is what Modernity is all about. From the ideal Man of Leonardo da Vinci, in proportion with the world and the regularity of Pythagorean geometry, to the modular Man of Le Corbusier and the wilder excesses of twentieth-century experiments in arcane areas of research such as the precise amount of worktop space necessary to allow the average housewife to prepare the average meal for an average size family, the notion of progress has been inextricably linked to measuring things – to an attempt to find, as accurately as possible, the data that confirm the mathematical regularity of all human activity. From a strictly commercial point of view, 100 per cent accuracy and a sound underlying thesis are unimportant. Anything above about 75 per cent is accurate enough and ensures that you will make more money than your competitors; the remaining 25 per cent doesn't really matter. Whilst apparently successful short-term plans can be pursued in certain areas – perhaps producing a limited range of clothing sizes or not bothering at all with left-handed scissors – in the long term, and particularly in the areas which have a substantial effect on the lives of others, there remains the 25 per cent of people who just don't fit into the rigorously determined dimensions of the optimal living space. Inevitably, a small percentage of this group will react by trashing the aforesaid optimally sized living space. Not everyone likes to have assumptions made about themselves.

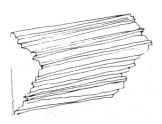

This regularised world of defined volumes and predetermined movements first appears in Julian Opie's block sculptures of 1991 and 1992, although there is an element of this in the earlier series of aluminium and glass frames and cabinets, which, through their relation to shop fittings and display cases, can be seen as structures intended to generate certain movement and behaviour. Works such as *It is believed that some dinosaurs could run faster than a cheetah*, 1991, echo the spaces of microprocessor architecture and mimic modernist city planning. They are laid out on a floor plan that could resemble anything from a Mondrian painting to a bookshelf unit from *Ikea*, and the walls of the blocks which define the channels running through the sculpture are colour coded for ease of orientation. An awareness of this coding allows the viewer to create a mental map of the routes of passageways and the position of the blocks while walking around the sculpture and looking into it from the different vantage points that are offered. Given enough effort, the pathways and obstructions resolve themselves completely. The white block sculptures are even more transparent in this respect: the roads through works such as *In order to cut glass it is necessary to score a line one molecule deep*, 1991, are angled and simply slice up the space, never encountering a single obstruction. As we move around the sculpture the view through to the other side is plain. The blocks themselves no longer block; they are just space fillers with the same matt white colour and texture as the gallery walls that surround them.

In contrast, the column sculptures that Opie produced at the same period are far less simple to resolve, and intentionally so. The 'columns' are conglomerations of decorative moulding strips – the antithesis of the modernist rectilinearity of the block sculptures – and as such, their volume and exact shape cannot be grasped. Their forms have both a slightly industrial and an organic flavour – like taking the coastline of Iceland as a template for a plastic extrusion. The extreme complexity of the surface that winds around the column, cutting in, projecting and occasionally doubling back on itself, keeps the eye so occupied in trying to determine what is

going on that there is no chance of methodically working out its true form. Some of the column sculptures, like the block pieces, are colour coded, but in this instance the attempt at clarification only serves to complicate matters further. The optical projection of some colours is often at odds with their real depth and areas of moulding appear to recede or project when in fact they are doing the opposite.

At moments like these, it feels as if the best way to grasp the substance of what is being looked at would be to see it in plan form; but that is not possible as the height of the columns hides their tops from view. This sense of frustration is echoed in the titles of many of the sculptures: *There are 60,000 miles of veins, arteries and capillaries in the human body (II)*, 1991, or *The Great Pyramid of Cheops contains enough stone to build a low wall around the whole of France*, 1991, which suggests the type of fact that is intended not only to amaze, but also to help in the visualisation of something not immediately apparent by presenting the information in a different, more legible form.

One of the characteristics of the block sculptures is that the channels which cut through them, although real and very visible, are not physically accessible: they are too narrow to allow passage. Walking around the work, however, encourages a mental projection into these interior spaces. This aspect of the work appears literally, if that is the right word, in the more recent series of road paintings. In works such as *Imagine you are driving* (2), 1993, the central focus is to do with exactly what the title implies: a notion of movement and an imaginative projection on the part of the viewer. What is presented is not a physical space, but an apparently time-based sequence of images of a three-lane motorway. Motorways are only for serious drivers – no learners, pedestrians or motorcycles under 50cc allowed. They fulfil one of the modern world's dreams of idealised transport. Almost anyone can go anywhere fast (as long as you want to go somewhere that is on the motorway). The range of options is narrow and decisions are, in essence, limited to junction numbers: you cannot stop, turn around or follow your whims but only exit at these

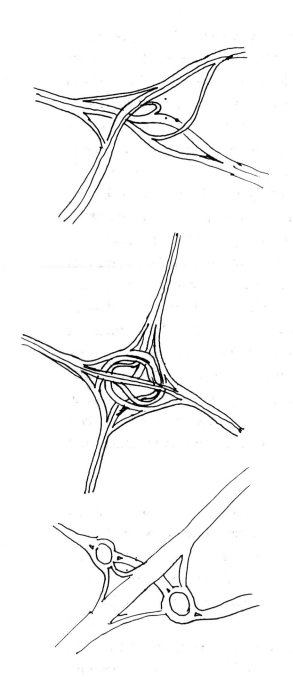

designated points. Motorways are for people who plan journeys. The motorway itself is not really a place: the immediate vista, the one on which the driver, at least, is supposed to concentrate, is predictable in the extreme. White lines, tarmac and endless grass verges provide the main visual stimuli, punctuated by the occasional bridge or flyover looming into view from a spot on the horizon. The sensation of weightlessness that comes into being when travelling over a certain speed reinforces this strange sense of unreality. Looking through a windscreen at a slowly changing yet strictly defined view is virtually the same experience as playing a computer driving game. There is more at stake, but unless you collide with a hostile object it is hard to appreciate the reality of high speed travel.

Some of Opie's most recent works have involved images and animated sequences constructed on computer. In one of these a camera tracks through the interior pathways of a complex block sculpture, providing a walk-through experience that is not possible with the real works. Like the block sculptures, however, this virtual sculpture allows only a limited degree of access, whilst appearing perfectly accessible: it appears to reveal the secrets of the 'real' sculpture, but the information it provides is beyond the viewers' control. In general, computer animation and computer simulation involve a particular vanity in trying to recreate the world: an exercise in futility for which the only motive can be a desire for complete control. The Victorians had their train sets, we have *Sim City*. Renaissance painters such as Uccello spent considerable time on perspective studies, from small-scale still-lifes to full-blown, historical figure compositions; perhaps we are reliving a Renaissance dream of complete comprehension and a desire to re-invent the world – or is it that we never let go of the aspirations in the first place and have modelled our world around them? In contrast to Opie's very pared-down use of the medium, the everyday computer graphics of the present, as is visible from television advertising, are at a similar stage of development to the first flush of success in Renaissance perspectival experiments.

Opie's recent paintings, sculptures and computer-generated images share something with the cartoon-like skin of his earliest painted sculptures. Their clarity and completeness is reminiscent of the ideal world in which Hergé's hero Tintin moves. Sharing Opie's preoccupation with the mechanisms of the modern world, the vast majority of Tintin's adventures involve travel – some of them *only* involve travel – and in the rare instances when he can be persuaded to stay at home, this situation is accompanied by a major technological advance, such as the invention of colour television by his colleague, Professor Calculus. When Tintin sets out by car, ship, train and plane into another culture and another adventure, every detail of his travel experience – train stations, airport departure lounges and hotel rooms – is meticulously described. Everything that Tintin travels in or on is at the pinnacle of contemporary technology: Italian sports car, electric train or swing-winged jet, all are rendered lovingly in precise detail. When Tintin ventures to the moon he does so unimpeded by the fact that space travel is yet to come, and reaches his destination in a rocket modelled on the results of German World War Two jet research. Tintin's acceptance of the world and his neutrality of stance are what mark him as the Modern Man: while his companions struggle with technology, blundering about in an attempt to make a world they don't feel entirely in control of perform their bidding, Tintin is at home with the system as it invisibly performs its functions and serves his needs.

Opie's work inhabits an environment which, like Tintin's, is an almost virtual world: it has no real texture, no age and no sense of decay. In Tintin's everlasting present, the sense of a place so real it is unreal is overpowering. The blocks of flat, uniform colour that describe this environment and the unwavering black lines of constant thickness that bound the forms of his own body as much as the objects he encounters transform everything into the representation of an ideal – but an ideal that has been made concrete. Everything is always new, always clean and always visible. Opie's recent paintings and the sculptures of building types – castles and

townhouses, for example – that represent sites of human activity and a generic past, have this same restraint and clarity which somehow renders them inescapably tangible yet distinctly unreal. There is, throughout Opie's work, a perplexing combination of clarity and resolvability, in which objects and situations are easily grasped and conceptualised, and yet this process is accompanied by a gradual discovery of the qualities that make this representation of the world different from perceived reality and experience. Opie's earliest painted sculptures contain what could be described as a narrative element: the objects depicted are predominantly items that are used, such as tools, furniture, food and clothes. They have an implied past and future and contain a sense of having been handled, creased or manipulated through human activity, and this is reflected in their less than pristine appearance. The later sculpture exists outside this realm: its finish is immaculate and unblemished by use. The most recent computer-generated work will, thanks to the digital nature of its construction, retain this quality indefinitely and remain as a constant temporal present.

There is, perhaps, an element of nostalgia in all of this: like flicking back through the pages of *Life* magazines of the 1950s and 1960s, with their advertisements for refrigerators, cars and assorted domestic appliances suspended in a state of perpetual newness; there is a sense of certainty that accompanies this past which is comparable to the certainties sought through mathematical quantifying of the world. Looking back at the modern world of the immediate post-war period, there is a sense that if one could project oneself into this space and time events would unfold with an inevitable predictability – like the motorway vista looming into view. It is this age of confidence, in which progress would make a better life for all, that is hinted at obliquely in Opie's references to early consumer appliances, in the aluminium sculptures, and in the purist modernity of the blocks. Where better, then, for the work to be situated than in the South Bank Centre, where, in the 1950s and for this country at least, the Modern Age began with the Festival of Britain?

23G/57
1990, enamel on zintex
120 × 280 × 128 cm

A 199/6
1989, zintex, aluminium, tinted glass,
enamel
24 panels, 188 × 324 × 405 cm

There are 60,000 miles of veins,
arteries and capillaries in a human body
1991, house paint on wood
141 × 207 × 29 cm

The Great Pyramid of Cheops
contains enough stone to build a low
wall around the whole of France
1991, oil paint on wood
198 × 267 × 30 cm

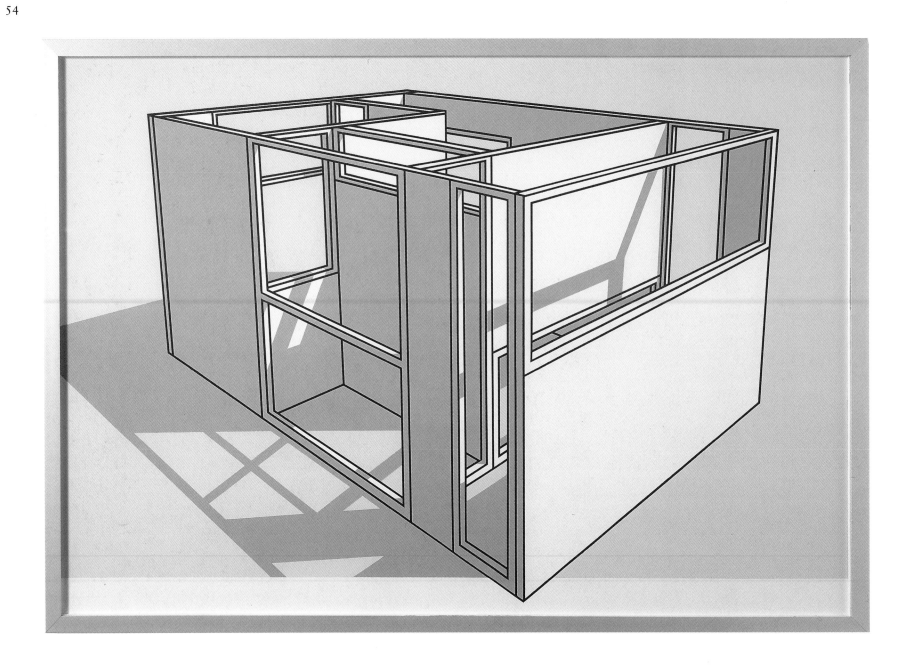

Painting of HA 45/11
1991, acrylic on wood, glass and
aluminium
87.5 × 126 × 5 cm

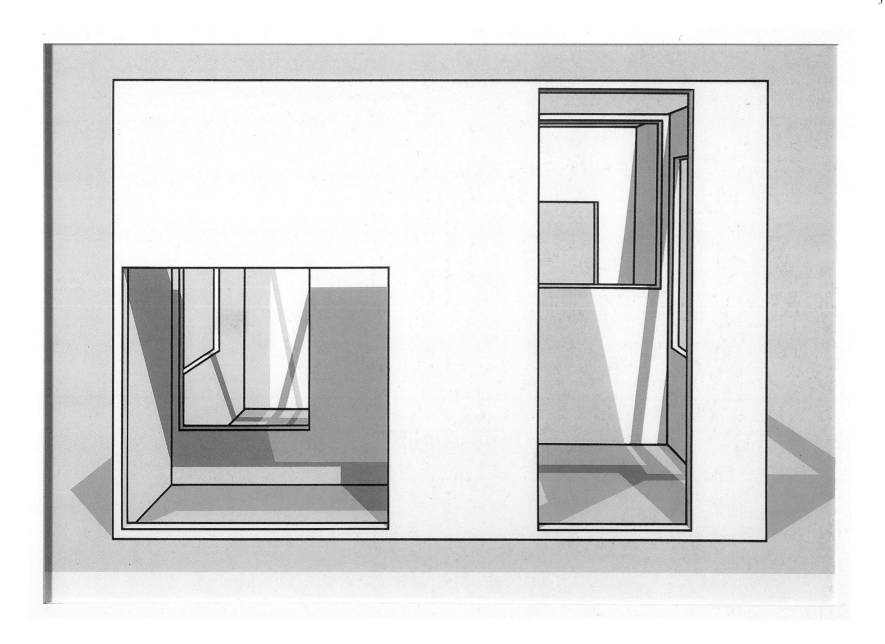

Painting of D/889 E
1991, acrylic on wood, glass and
aluminium
87.5 × 126 × 5 cm

HA/45-11
1990, paint on wood, glass
198 × 289.5 × 208 cm

Imagine you are climbing
1992, paint on wood
220 × 200 × 200 cm

It is believed that some dinosaurs
could run faster than a cheetah
1991, emulsion on wood
200 × 200 × 280 cm

In order to cut glass it is necessary to
score a line one molecule deep
1991, emulsion on wood
196 × 240 × 200 cm

Painting of It is believed that some
dinosaurs could run faster than a cheetah
1991, aluminium, glass, acrylic on wood
89 × 127 × 4 cm

Painting of In order to cut glass it is necessary
to score a line one molecule deep
1991, aluminium, glass, acrylic on wood
89 × 127 × 4 cm

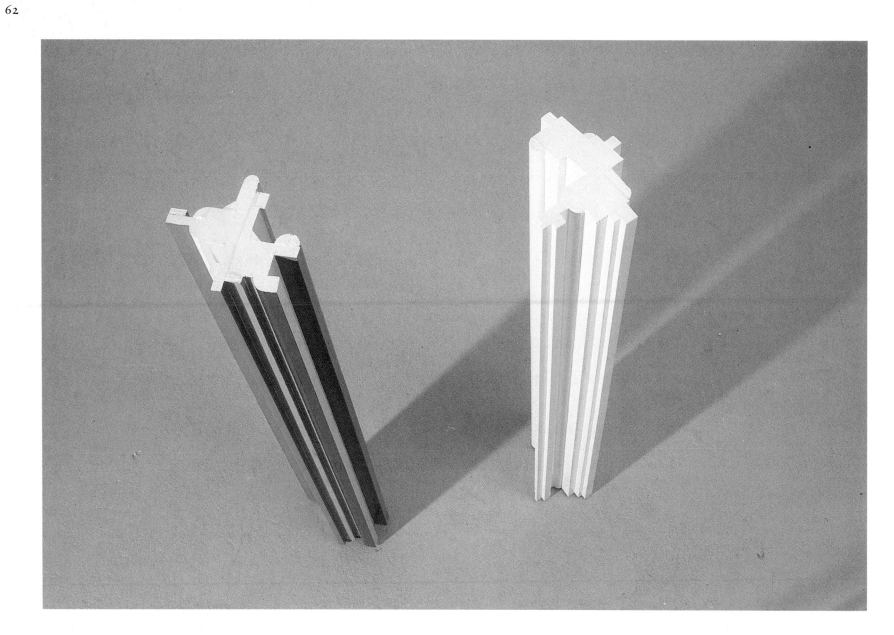

Installation, Primo Piano, Rome,
1991: foreground: There are
1800 electrical storms in the
earth's atmosphere at any
one time
1991, gloss paint on wood
230 × 55 × 61 cm

background: The average speed of
a car in London is slower than
that of equestrian traffic at the
turn of the century
1991, gloss paint on wood
230 × 55 × 61 cm

opposite: models for the two works
above

Wren's Great Model of St. Paul's Cathedral
Photo © Woodmansterne

Mrs James Ward Thorne standing before her Louis XVI bedroom at an exhibition of her first set of miniature rooms, early 1930s.

Photograph courtesy of The Art Institute of Chicago

Giorgio De Chirico, The Disquieting Muses, 1917
oil on canvas
97.1 × 66 cm
© DACS 1993

Rehearsing Realities:
Julian Opie's Scaled Buildings

Lynne Cooke

I.

'I would not have the models too exactly finished, nor too delicate and neat, but plain and simple, more to be admired for the contrivance of the inventor than the hand of the workman.' *Alberti*, BOOK II, DE RE AEDIFICATORIA.

From Michelangelo's sketch models, first roughly executed in clay then refined in wood, to the diminutive colossus, some twenty feet long, built by Christopher Wren in the 1660s when designing St. Paul's Cathedral, historical models continue to exercise an enormous fascination.[1] Yet often now they are more admired for their craftsmanship and their perfection as complete, hermetic miniature worlds than for any historical information they may vouchsafe. In this way, they have taken on affinities with another category of models, that of tiny period-architecture replicas built expressly for display purposes, among which the celebrated Thorne Rooms at the Art Institute of Chicago are pre-eminent.

From the time of the Egyptians onwards models have played a crucial role in developing and clarifying the conceptions of architects and builders, as well as in the presentation of their ideas to clients. Recently, however, as witnessed by the escalating costs devoted to the construction of these elaborate but minute sketches, the propaganda value of persuasion has overswayed the use of the model as the site of invention, its principal former role. Reacting against this contemporary tendency to use presentation models as narrative rather than conceptual tools, Peter Eisenman and several other architects mounted an exhibition in New York in 1976

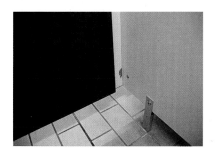

titled 'Idea as Model'.[2] In his essay in the accompanying catalogue, Christian Hubert adumbrates the 'model's condition of being just outside the limits of building'. 'Perhaps the model concretizes the ontic condition of the project', he speculates. 'It exists as desire – in a kind of atopia, if not utopia. It holds out the promise of inhabitation, even if it does not fully afford it.' 'For the space of the model lies on the border between representation and actuality', he continues. 'Like the frame of a painting, ... the model is neither wholly inside nor wholly outside, neither pure representation nor transcendent object. It claims a certain autonomous objecthood, yet this condition is always incomplete. The model is always a model *of*. The *desire* of the model is to act as a simulacrum of another object, as a surrogate which allows for imaginative occupation.'[3]

Speculating that the model is 'perhaps the articulation of representation itself, which seeks a resuscitation of a "reality" beyond the limits of the sign', he quotes Jean Baudrillard: 'The sign is haunted by the nostalgia for overcoming its *own* convention, that of being arbitrary. It is haunted by the idea of *total motivation*. It aims at the real as its beyond and abolition. But it cannot jump over its own shadow: this real is produced and reproduced by the sign itself. It is only its *horizon*. Reality is the fantasy by which the sign protects itself indefinitely from the destruction that haunts it.'[4]

Contrasting with the mimetic simulation of the architectural model is the differently constructed surrogate of the doll's house. Unlike the architectural model it seeks a norm: it is, typically, standardised in character rather than exceptional in design. Originally devised for adult amusement, the doll's house offers the promise of an infinitely profound interiority. In its grandest, quintessential forms, epitomised in the magnificent example made for Queen Mary in 1920, it is designed for display, that is, to be seen rather than engaged, to be consumed by the eye instead of being played with. A sanctuary as well as a site of fantasy, it offers a complete, hermetic world – as do all miniatures, among which it constitutes a distinctive subset.[5]

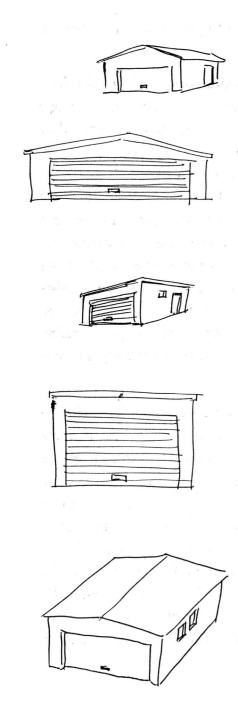

Julian Opie's recent sculptural models seem to site themselves somewhat apart from these two modes, though remaining nonetheless obliquely related to them. Cursory in their fabrication like certain historical models, they nevertheless differ from architectural models *per se* in being generic instead of determined by, and determining of, individual prototypes. Their forms tend to derive from those building typologies that are governed primarily by functional and technological needs: the basic components and configurations of castles and fortresses, for example, are determined by technological developments; those of cathedrals by liturgical requirements. Only when the technology, or faith, evolves radically do such forms alter significantly, quickly becoming redundant: prior to that, individual variations are minor in character, few in number and, hence, inconsequential to the typology as a whole. Like many functional designs, these standardised configurations, too, are anonymous, for the conventions peculiar to each idiom usually evolved slowly over time. The historical prototypes for Opie's sculptures are thus not individual examples but categories of examples. Like their medieval predecessors, Opie's Gothic models might also be described as *pro forma* and *pro exempla,* because they capture the *veritas* of a project without offering blueprints for its execution.

Tellingly, Opie's buildings have no interiors. The architectural model, by contrast, normally offers a foretaste of the proposed spaces of inhabitation, whilst the doll's house focuses on the interior in preference to the exterior as the site of imaginative identification. Moreover, the stripped-down simplicity and overt hollowness of Opie's works means that unlike these other types of models his can be taken in at a glance. Instantly graspable, the straightforwardness of their construction accords with the details of their iconography, so familiar as to be accommodated almost without attention. Hubert proposes that in the case of contemporary architects 'the craft of building models may be seen as the displacement and condensation of the craft of building, an attempt to recover the aura of the work by fetishising the

facticity of surrogate objects'.[6] Opie, however, eschews this possibility by employing an apparently artless level of fabrication.

Yet their very blankness coupled with an assertive oddness of scale makes them surprisingly compelling. Never so vast that they cannot be moved by a single person, they read as simultaneously big *and* small. In relation to what they represent in actuality they are, of course, tiny: however, in relation to the category of miniatures and its subsets – models, toys or period rooms – they appear incongruously large. Although varying considerably in literal size, common to all this group of Opie's works is the fact that none has an establishable, measurable relationship to any single prototype as do 'real' models. They are, in consequence, strangely scale-less. In mentally adjusting his or her viewpoint when confronting each piece, the viewer inevitably recalls Alice and Gulliver, also subject to worlds which wilfully shrank and grew. The resulting effect of estrangement is reinforced by the deracinated nature of their existence: the space that each occupies remains somehow indeterminate; and each merely skims the ground, sitting slightly above it on concealed feet.

The desire Opie's works mobilise is thus of another order from that pertaining to miniatures in general, for desire rooted in the interiority of the subject produces nostalgic reverie, and longing. In Opie's art, by contrast, desire has its source in a quite other notion of play, one generated when the commonplace and quotidian, the blatantly ordinary, is pushed to an extreme, or inverted, as in a game. In his much discussed critique of minimal art, Michael Fried singled out for attack a number of qualities, including its blatant hollowness: 'Like Judd's Specific Objects and Morris' gestalts or unitary forms, [Tony] Smith's cube is *always* of further interest', he asserted; 'one never feels that one has come to the end of it. It is inexhaustible, however, not because of any fullness – *that* is the inexhaustibility of art – but because there is nothing there to exhaust. It is endless the way a road might be: if it were circular, for example.'[7]

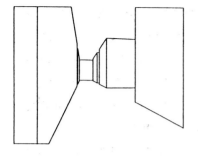

Opie shares neither Baudrillard's dystopian vision nor Fried's disdain for theatricality in art. He values differently the possibility of an articulation of representation in and for itself. In accepting that reality may remain forever a fantasy, the sign now refuses to attempt to resuscitate that reality, privileging the domain of play over that of actuality. Sidestepping the overworked and increasingly vacant notion of depth which preoccupied Fried, and others, he opts for the surface, a decision which does not, however, consign him to superficiality. For he discerns in a kind of numb aloofness, 'dumb' simplicity and low resolution, something of the measure of adequacy that characterises much of everyday peripheral experience. Aesthetic experiences, especially those generated by high art, are usually calibrated in terms of degrees of innovation and originality. By contrast, constrained as it often is into predigested and ersatz forms, the ordinary and familiar has a wholly different potential for affectivity, one which may be measured in terms of estrangement and displacement. 'The only explanation I can think of for wanting to eat bland food,' the artist stated in a recent interview, '... [is] a desire to match the sense of distance you feel between the way you understand the external world and your emotional response to it'.[8] Opie's sculptural models invoke not a particularised experience, as do the singular instances surviving from the past, which purport to present architecture rather than represent it, but the *idea* of a kind of experience, something at once more generalised and more abstract.

II.

'To toy with something is to manipulate it, to try it out within sets of contexts none of which is determinate.' *Susan Stewart*, ON LONGING.

The ground behind the two mannequins who occupy centre stage in *The Disquieting Muses* (1917) rises steeply, terminating in what at first appears to be an odd conjunction of buildings: to the left an industrial structure and two towering chimneys; to the right a crenellated castle. Yet since it is unclear precisely where

these buildings stand in space and what their exact relation is to the vast but precipitous mid-ground plane, this ambience takes on an uncannily disturbing character. Here, as so often in De Chirico's art, the mysteriousness of his vision owes as much to its unsettling *mise-en-scène* as to its agents, who, whether transfixed figures or immobile statues, are invariably cast adrift in indefinable, incommensurable, and seemingly untraversable spaces, where time stands still. In certain of his paintings the gigantic buildings, more akin to scenographic flats than concrete realities, loom ominously over the figures; in others they are revealed *in potentia,* as building blocks, false façades, and standardised units, reminiscent of the contents of a child's construction set. That De Chirico should devise this unsettling world – the world of dreams, fantasies and phobias – from standardised, generic building types, among which the castle, the smokestack, the lighthouse, the arcade and the factory predominate, is highly significant.[9]

But it is as much due to the character of his spatial constructions as to that of his built environments that unease sets in. Irrationality insidiously breaks through what should be a coherent, cohesive three-dimensional world, portrayed by means of a unified, one-point, perspectival system, distorting without thoroughly destroying. Unlike the totally ethereal optical spaces – spaces which, in lacking all coordinates, become unmappable – beloved by his peers, Miró, Mattà and Tanguy, De Chirico clung to a traditional plastic space, albeit one that in its vulnerability to arbitrary disruptive superventions became dislocated and disorienting.

For the Surrealists it was the originality of the Italian artist's vision of the enigmatic and the uncanny that proved so captivating. In recent decades the ubiquity of his oeuvre – the product of widespread fame and endless reproduction – has infused its signal strangeness with a familiarity. When encountering one of De Chirico's well-known paintings a pleasurable sense of recognition now informs the mystery, often not dispelling it but, paradoxically, adding to its charm. A similar kind of pleasure attends the re-viewing of early science fiction films where the

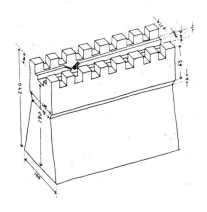

passage of time reveals their now outmoded special effects and formulaic conventions with particular clarity – once again without necessarily detracting from the spectator's engagement. Hindsight and familiarity need not, however, breed nostalgia, for the viewer retains the option of suspending disbelief in order to re-enter what is patently a make-believe world, and, simultaneously, of staying aloof, knowingly attentive to its conventions. Through this dislocation the work takes on something of the character of a sign: when it has become a representation of itself the signified is, if not wholly absent, at least at one remove. As in the case of architectural models, the viewer ends up dealing as much with simulacral experience as with aesthetic immediacy.

Edgar Allen Poe once persuasively argued that a certain quotient of definite indefiniteness was integral to the staffage of dreams, fantasies and phobias. This quality informs the built environments not only of De Chirico, but of Katharina Fritsch and Julian Opie, as it does Poe's own: all are imbued with a deceptively deadpan, lapidary commonplaceness. Far from precluding undifferentiated textures and substances, Poe's notion of concreteness seems to invite it, for they accord perfectly with a generic architectural iconography. As in the case of her *Dark Green Tunnel* (1979) and *Grey Mill* (1979), Fritsch usually presents her small-scale three-dimensional motifs on pedestals that resemble merchandise stands, thereby removing them from the realm of the ordinary to that of the miniature, the toy and the keepsake. By entering the arena of play and make-believe they become metaphors for the interior space and time of the perceiving subject. Opie, by contrast, sets his model buildings assertively in the viewer's space, inviting direct confrontation. Yet because of the undecidability of their scale, and the indeterminate tenor of the spaces they occupy (or enclose), proximity does not ensure intimacy; their identities remain elusively ambiguous. Their materiality – their quiddity – is undermined by the even coat of gloss paint which imparts an all-over abstractness to their surfaces; their subject matter is generalised by the absence

of a certain level of detail; and their objecthood is compromised, for although indubitably physical entities they are, nonetheless, also illusory representations. Situated on the boundary between pictorialism and physicality, locating their concerns at the crossroads of actuality and allusion, reality and fantasy, they invite the suspension of the real in favour of play.

Opie's interest in De Chirico is differently grounded from Fritsch's, in that he is less concerned with recapturing and savouring fundamental, formative experiences than in scrutinizing those states of detachment and distance at the heart of not only the familiar and quotidian, but of much that typifies the realms of the fantastical, the virtual and the fictive. Nevertheless, Julian Heynen's acute observation that Fritsch is preoccupied with 'the simultaneous embeddedness and distance of a symbolically overworked image' is also applicable to Opie, though he pursues this in somewhat idiosyncratic fashion.[10] Whereas she seeks to recapture a childhood sense of wonder through epiphanic encounters, he subjects the realities underpinning states of make-believe, play or fantasy to wry scrutiny. Less earnest in his faith in images than Fritsch, and highly sceptical of the desire to re-awaken an unprejudiced eye, he examines all via a kind of ludic interrogation. His scaled buildings remain, in consequence, quizzically and equivocally poised at the intersection of various competing realities.

III.

'The process of reading things as simulations but knowing at the same time that they are real is quite central to my work'. *Julian Opie*

'What does exaggeration, as a mode of signification, exaggerate?' Susan Stewart cannily asks in her brilliant study of the miniature and the gigantic, titled *On Longing*.[11] The hyperreality which Umberto Eco sees as quintessential to the experience of American reality might be read on the one hand as inflated, hollow or

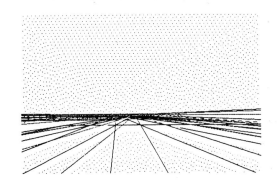

theatrical, or alternatively as serving to create a stage for the playful, oneiric and fantastical.[12] In his analyses of travel and tourism Eco considers the theme park the American equivalent of the European historic landmark. The spread of mass tourism in Europe results in a succession of coordinated streamlined interchangeable movements between what are increasingly identical, because increasingly mediated, places of historic interest: and landmarks become reduced to points of orientation. The American sites, by contrast, declare their artefactuality and artificiality from the outset, and in ways that celebrate these very attributes. Both types of site, however, increasingly take on the character of simulacra, of signs without precise referents: these generic typologies, including, notably, walled towns, fortresses, mediaeval cathedrals, classical amphitheatres, rustic farmhouses and light-towers find their New World counterparts at Graceland and Wonderland.

Like a road movie which reduces all sights outside the vehicle to generically interchangeable sites, so the endless dreamlike circuits of Fantasyland or Tomorrowland are landscaped with stereotypical examples of whatever architecture is deemed appropriate to that imaginary world. In fantasy as in reality minimal information is all that is required to read the periphery, because it is the act of travelling itself which has become of central importance. Something similar occurs in those video and computer games where driving is again the subject, the road central and the material on its borders liminal to the experience of circumnavigating the course. Such modes of travelling may be better defined as excursions rather than as journeys. If the journey encompasses lived experience the excursion evades it, and escapes it, Susan Stewart argues. 'The excursion is a carnival mode, but an alienated one,' she contends: 'its sense of return is manufactured out of resignation and necessity.'[13]

In his introduction to an anthology which, in part, explores the potential models of spatialisation which the new digital technologies make possible, Michael Benedict stresses that '*space itself* is something not necessarily physical: rather it is a

"field of play" for all information, only one of whose manifestations is the gravitational and electromagnetic field of play we live in, and that we call the real world'.[14] Given the malleability of virtual space, and the magnitude of the task facing cyberspace architects required to design electronic edifices and data cartographies for vast and rapidly expanding new needs, the spatial constructions in many contemporary video games seem very unsophisticated, almost primitive. Faced with almost unlimited possibilities for a novel, open, virtual architecture, the trend to employ a regressive, that is, old-fashioned, mode of representing space for the exercise of play and pleasure is at first sight unexpected. Yet it is precisely this relatively primitive form of simulated realism which largely accounts for Julian Opie's interest in home video games. To him it recalls the architectural and spatial constructions found in late medieval and early Renaissance painting, as well as in De Chirico's fraught visions. Significantly, players range from the young to the adult, and sophistication provides no inherent advantages.

These simulations might be compared, too, with the work of Aldo Rossi, not only with his drawings of imaginary urbanscapes but also with certain of his realised projects. Rossi's deceptively simple, profoundly archaic vision of architecture reveals both strong and affectionate connections to historical tradition, alongside a reverence for Etienne-Louis Boullée in whose work, he believes, 'use and decoration are one'.[15] Unlike the architecture of many of his contemporaries who draw on the iconography of the past in order to historicise and appropriate traditional motifs, Rossi's bold configurations of simple stereometric forms betray a strong attachment to indigenous and vernacular modes. The seductive charm of his vision as much as his fondness for Pinocchio as a sort of talisman betrays a childlike playfulness that informs the most distinctive of his structures.

Formerly castigated for executing numerous versions of his more memorable paintings, for what was scathingly deemed 'the production of reproductions', De Chirico today looks uncannily prescient and prophetic.[16] For in prefiguring the

current vogue for rehearsing realities he chose to site his oneiric vision in the old-fashioned domain of the make-believe. It is no coincidence that common to his art and that of Rossi, Fritsch, Opie and others are the graphics, iconography, forms and gestalts that exemplify the culture of (modern) childhood, its aporias as well as its harmonies. In the deceptive simplicities of this diminutive and therefore manipulable version of experience, a version that is domesticated and protected from contamination, lie the first instances of realities which will be rehearsed again and again in an unassuagable need to know the world by constructing it.

Notes:

1   John Wilton-Ely, 'The Architectural Model: 1. English Baroque', *Apollo*, vol.88, October 1968, pp.250–259. Note too should be taken of the imaginary architectural constructions of such artists as the West African Aboudramane, and Bodys Isek Kingelez from Zaire, although these sacrifice objecthood to representation.

2   *Idea as Model,* The Institute for Architecture and Urban Studies, New York, 1976.

3   Christian Hubert, 'The Ruins of Representation', *Idea as Model,* The Institute for Architecture and Urban Studies/Rizzoli, New York, 1980, p.17.

4   Jean Baudrillard, *Pour une Economie Politique du Signe,* (Paris, 1973), quoted in Hubert, op. cit., p.19.

5   Around 1980 Robert Gober made a series of highly detailed sculptures akin to doll's houses that explored issues of domestic relations.

6   Hubert, op. cit., p.17.

7   Fried, 'Art and Objecthood', reprinted in Gregory Battcock, ed., *Minimal Art: A Critical Anthology,* E.P. Dutton, New York, 1968, pp.143–144. Fried is here referring ironically to Tony Smith's famous account of a car ride at night. Minimalism has been a constant touchstone and source of dialogue for Opie's work from the mid-'eighties onwards.

8   Quoted in James Roberts, 'Tunnel Vision', *Frieze,* May 1993, p.33.

9   Compare for example the castle in *The Disquieting Muses* with that in Filippo De Pisis' outline sketch of Ferrara in his *La Città delle 100 Meraviglie;* both foreshadow contemporary *topoi* for castles in current children's primers.

10   Julian Heynen, 'Speculations on Trucks, Cemeteries, Foxes, and Other Images', *Parkett,* no.25, 1990, p.54. Fritsch is not alone in this aspect of her aesthetic: the work of Martin Honert and Stephan Balkenhol, amongst others, is similarly motivated.

11   Susan Stewart, *On Longing: Narratives of the Miniature, the Gigantic, the Souvenir, the Collection,* Duke University Press, Durham and London, 1993, p.ix.

12   Umberto Eco, 'Travels in Hyperreality', *Travels in Hyperreality,* Harcourt Brace Jovanovich, San Diego, New York, London, 1986, pp.1–58.

13   Susan Stewart, op. cit., p.60

14   Michael Benedict, 'Introduction', *Cyberspace: First Steps,* Massachusetts Institute of Technology, Cambridge, Mass., 1991, p.20.

15   Quoted in Karen Stein, 'Il Celeste della Madonna', in *Aldo Rossi Architecture 1981–1991,* edited by Morris Adjmi, Princeton Architectural Press, New York, 1991, p.271.

16   Certain of these critiques proposed not only an aesthetic decline but a moral turpitude, as seen in the polemics surrounding the De Chirico retrospective held at the Museum of Modern Art in New York in 1982, where curator William Rubin ended his essay with an unexpectedly personalised apologia, which damned most of the artist's late production. Accompanying this denunciation was a dramatic visual finale, a double-page spread of eighteen versions of *The Disquieting Muses* which De Chirico had made between 1945 and 1964. That the effect was Warhol-like was no coincidence for this American's late work, too, was then viewed as an ethical as well as aesthetic sell-out by many, not least MoMA itself. *Giorgio De Chirico,* The Museum of Modern Art, New York, 1982, pp.73–75.

Operation Atopia

Michael Newman

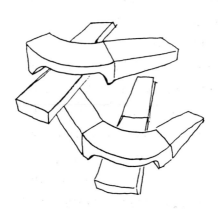

'Virtual worlds are non-places. But the body can never be a non-body. This confrontation between non-places and real bodies is the crux of the problem of the virtual.' *Philippe Quéau*[1]

Opie's work needs to be understood in relation to a change in the concept of art practice, or at least in one of the models on which we base our idea of what an artist does, and to a concomitant mutation in the quality and experience of modernity.

To describe Julian Opie's work as 'sculpture' serves to draw attention to the late 20th-century phenomenon of the pictorialisation of three-dimensional experience. If, in computer-generated virtual reality, image and space are, in principle if not yet in practice, supposed to be entirely interchangeable, Opie works in the opposite direction, prising apart image and spatial object, or integrating them so completely that they change places and begin to break apart again.[2] A good example of the latter would be the 'road' paintings of 1993 which appear more solid, more real than a photograph, or than the actual experience of driving along a motorway. Their titles, such as *Imagine you are driving at night*, are partly ironic, in that this imagined scene is constituted by reference to interactive computer graphics, interpolating the 'driver' in a fixed position. The supposed freedom of imagination, for the Romantics a 'gift of Nature', has become a means of control by expert systems. However, Opie's work also demonstrates that attempts at institutional control of the gaze, and the technological modelling of experience, end up, through their inevitable moments of failure, reminding us of the irreducibility of the body in perception, of finitude and the contingencies which the phantasies involved in information technology dream of overcoming.[3]

Generic objects and the operative approach to art

The allusion to a historic genre of art-making such as 'sculpture' should thus serve as counterpoint rather than as legitimation – not least since Opie's work situates itself in the modern tradition of the break with such generic distinctions which goes back at least as far as Duchamp. Opie is no more and no less a 'sculptor' than is the American 'minimalist' artist Donald Judd: where Judd sought to make what he called 'specific objects' which were 'neither painting nor sculpture', Opie makes 'generic objects', whether these are produced by three-dimensional fabrication, by painting, or by a combination of the two. With the idea of 'generic objects', genre is applied to an object-type rather than to a mode of production. Opie's displacement and manipulation of the generic characteristics of design presentation are apparent in the catalogue of his exhibition at the Kohji Ogura Gallery in Nagoya, Japan in 1991, and the artist's book of the same year[4]: constructivist absolute space has become the flattened out, imagistic space of computer design, where commercial catalogue numbers become enigmatic ciphers in the margins. It is hard to decide whether the relation to commercial modes of presentation betrays the truth about contemporary art, or whether commercial generic images or illustrations are themselves becoming objects of aesthetic contemplation.

Opie takes up the transformation in the conception of what an artist does, initiated in different ways by the Constructivists and by Duchamp, and developed by the Minimalists among others since the 1960s. The shift in question is from a representationalist to an operative approach. Not that an 'operative' approach necessarily excludes representation and mimesis: rather, representation becomes a certain operation among other possibilities, thus losing its privilege. The artist operates on given materials (physical materials, images, language, etc.) in the broadest sense. Equally, the genres of traditional art, such as painting and sculpture, become merely options among a range of possible operations.

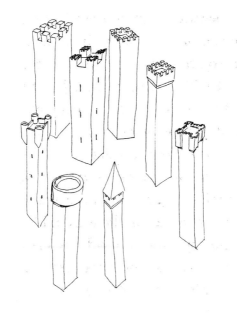

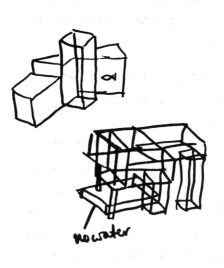

As a paradigm, the latest variant of this operative conception may be linked to technological and social developments. For example, in the field of design a computer offers a range of operations which may be performed on a basic figure, such as rotation, changes in scale, changes in colour, or the movement of elements. (Artistic operativity would have a metaphorical rather than a literal relation to such a model.) And in the mode of factory production, the role in the division of labour once taken by a number of workers each assigned to a particular task involving repetitive movements is now delegated to an operator who, through computers, controls, selects and varies the operations of the machines, making possible the programming of variations and even the manufacture of one-off products. A paradox of Opie's approach is that he combines an operative 'attitude' with an artisanal or workshop mode of production. Sometimes this deliberately inappropriate mode of production can be read off imperfections in the results, subverting the perfection of the technological object, but at other times it is implicit in the displacement of the focus of attention from that of the goal of a means-end relation to the non-functional 'aesthetic' standpoint.

The quasi-technological concept of the artist, far from being just an ultra- or post-modern phenomenon, brings the story of the aesthetic full circle, back to the ancient Greek idea of art as a form of *techne*.[5] And insofar as Opie's works involve a distancing from modern technological simulation and control, we are then faced, perhaps, not with a banal opposition of art and technology (since at their origin art and technology are fundamentally the same), but with the need to make distinctions between different possibilities inherent in the history of 'technology'.

The operative concept of art practice demands a critical approach to art with its own rigour. Considered synchronically, the various operations an artist performs amount in their interrelationships to a logic. Considered diachronically, the operations can be understood as a sequence of moves, or altogether as a single move with respect to the possibilities of the practice of art as perceived at a

particular time. The synchronic and diachronic approaches are interdependent on every level. For an operation to stand out as a significant move – that is, in a sense, for it to be recognised at all – requires a horizon of expectation on the part of the viewer which will have been historically formed, and will involve a reflection on history, including that of its own formation. (This kind of historical self-consciousness, itself a modern phenomenon, is probably a historical condition for the emergence of an operative approach.) But, conversely, the appreciation of the historical significance of an artist's project will depend on an understanding of the internal logic of their work. Without some, even minimal, gap between internal logic and historical horizon of expectation, artistic innovation would be impossible, but without the possibility of bridging that gap, the operations would remain incoherent and without significance (which does not exclude the possibility of randomness as a possible operation with its own meaning, as in the case of the work of John Cage).

Logic

I propose to begin with a brief account of the kinds of operations apparent in Opie's work to date. Taken together, and often coexisting in a single work, these amount to an internal logic which cuts across apparent differences in style and 'look'.

Appropriation. In its most basic sense, appropriation involves the taking over and re-presentation of already existing images or objects. Rather than a literal appropriation, as in the Duchampian 'found object' or the scavenging of photographic images characteristic of the early 1980s, Opie's procedure has tended towards the reproduction of generic types of object and image. This procedure applies not just to signs and things, but also to modes of making art, styles of design, etc., as in the 'Bauhaus fish tanks' (c.1981) of Opie's student days, where actual goldfish swam in transparent, partitioned spaces which anticipated, among other recent works, those of 1989 alluding to temporary exhibition stands. Other object-types are appropriated for the *Shelf Units* and *Column* sculptures using mouldings of 1991.

Displacement. In effect, appropriation is a mode of displacement. Displacement is more extensive than appropriation insofar as, for example, mimesis (imitation) can be understood as another mode of displacement. Thus the works of 1987–88 which resemble vents, refrigerators and display cabinets could be seen both as an imitative appropriation of a certain style of utility objects and of a characteristic cool, fetishistic surface finish, and their displacement into the gallery and into art.

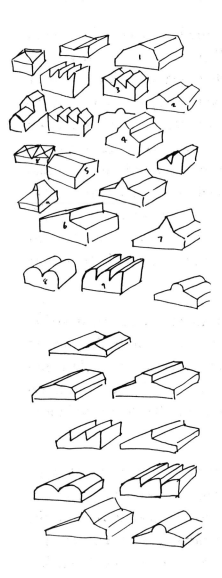

Modularisation. This category suggests the repetition, variation and interchangeability of basic units (even if the result is a fixed structure). The works of 1986 consisting of building-block units in painted steel, evoking the outer parts of cars or bits of architecture, would be one example, and others would be the various works taking the form of arrangements of blocks of 1991–92 and the differently scaled houses of *Imagine it's raining* (1992). Opie sometimes produces modularity as an effect rather than using it as a basis of production: a displacement of the modular from a functional to a perceptual role, as in the case of the works resembling prefabricated, partitioned offices or exhibition stands, such as *A 199/6* of 1989. In a recent group of works, *Imagine you can order these,* the variation inherent in modularisation has become an explicit element: each work consists of twelve units together with a number of proposed layouts (others can be added by whoever is taking the decision on a particular arrangement). Whereas previously Opie has played out the possible options of a given work-type across a number of different works, here he has included the different options within the same work. As in modularisation as a principle of organisation which extends beyond the field of design into, for example, education, the principle of identity has become programmed difference, difference integrated into a systemic whole. Choice is simultaneously proposed and controlled. These works' reference to play, to

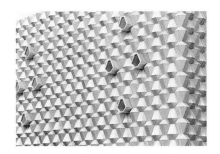

children's building blocks, highlights by contrast the extent to which, in modularisation, control functions through the illusion or spectacle of freedom.

Generic repetition and difference. Modules are the internal elements of a generic object. Generic objects are standardised object-types. Thus the artist can reproduce not a particular object (as for example in still-life) but those features which allow an object to be attributed to a particular genre of objects, which may be visible features rather than functions (thus operating as a displacement of 'normal' attribution). Or the process of 'rendering generic' can itself be imitated, thus inventing 'genres' of object internally to the oeuvre, which obviously requires production in series so that the generic repetition of identities can stand out against the differences. The *Column* sculptures of 1991 could be seen as an appropriation of available mouldings, an allusion to the Classical column, and even the invention of a new order of column. The white and the coloured Box works of 1991 would be a more pure, or 'purist', example.

Rescaling. This involves transformations of scale which detach the size of an object from a norm based on a privileged model, convention or the human body. Thus an early work of Opie's reproduced in three dimensions the equalisation of different-sized paintings found in a book of reproductions, and more recently, toy motor-racing circuits are enlarged in concrete, and works based on the shapes of houses and castles varied in scale.

None of these operations is neutral: most of them involve a mimicry of post-industrial modes of production, design and presentation. In some of Opie's most recent works this procedure is re-applied, anachronistically, to building types of the past such as castles, works which involve all the operations described above and serve to remind us of the experiences of exclusion and control common to a number of Opie's objects and images. To conceive the operative approach itself as a form of mimicry suggests that it is simultaneously defensive and an aggressive mode of

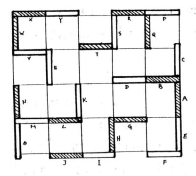

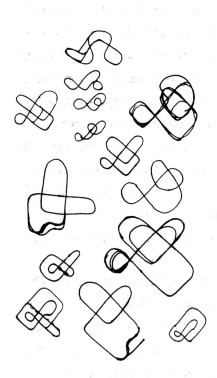

appropriation; the features – the physiognomy – of institutional control are taken over to become an object of play: that which manipulates the subject is manipulated in its turn, opening up the possibility of a degree of freedom and reflective knowledge achieved through perceptual self-awareness.

In addition, the very possibility of elaborating a series of operations in this way (there may be others) depends on a prior condition, which is simply that what an artist does, and what an artwork is, can no longer be taken for granted. The artist has to establish her or his own norms of procedure and principles of intelligibility (both of which may be selected or invented). These norms and principles will only be validated retrospectively.

The elaboration of an internal logic could lead to formalism. If Opie's work is not in the end formalist, this is because it involves a phenomenology as well as a logic. And insofar as this phenomenology concerns the phenomenal experience of a continuing process of modernisation, Opie's approach can be historically situated in relation to the tradition of modernist art as a narrative of reflective responses to the experience of Modernity. But, as we shall see, his work equally, and paradoxically, involves a shift in (relation to) the modernist project.

Phenomenology

It is important to distinguish between 'phenomenology' as it has been understood, and largely condemned, in Anglo-American art discourse since the 1960s – the contemplative experience of optical sensations – and its stricter philosophical sense, where phenomenology refers to the relation between the things that appear and their modes of disclosure, the 'how' of their appearance. Opie's work functions phenomenologically on the following levels:

The *materials* – taken in the broad sense of physical materials, forms, images, language (especially in the titles) – on which Opie operates carry over residues of the phenomenology of social life.

The *operations* performed on those materials involve a phenomenology of processes of production, circulation and consumption – of information as well as objects and images.

The *sites* in which the works appear (the art gallery, the museum) are related through the works' references to other sites together with their characteristic experiences (the showroom, the shopping mall and supermarket, the trade exhibition, the lobby, the airport, the motorway). These displacements foreground the interrelationship of institutional control and freedom with respect to the gaze: for example, the way in which the apparent transparency of corporate architecture conceals its real opacity,[6] and the way in which the 'freedom of the road' is subject to strict limits, and is indeed subject to total control just when those limits appear to have been suspended, as in a computer game. In the 1993 works based on model houses and castles, the model village – a somewhat anachronistic phantasy site – is abstracted and updated, showing how the omnipotent 'overview', which appears to have been perfected, for example, in satellite pictures, remains relative. But relative to what? Opie plays on the disjunction between two forms of relativity: a relativity based on relations internal to the system, but without a common measure (x is larger than a and smaller than b...), and another based on the human measure of embodiment and locatedness in space and time. However, although there may be no 'view from nowhere', we have become familiar with the experience of actual 'non-places': when 'nowhere' attains a location in space and time, 'somewhere' becomes just 'anywhere', as ubiquitous as a globally marketed brand-name product.

In Opie's work carried-over traces of social experience are played off against the 'pure', 'autonomous' handling of the experiences of space, form and colour characteristic of a certain conception of high Modernism. What is evoked is an irony or scepticism towards both which, however, is far from detached, but rather immersed in contemporary phenomena: an irony not of transcendence but of immanent oscillation and ambiguity concerning both the vantage point of the subject and the status of the object.

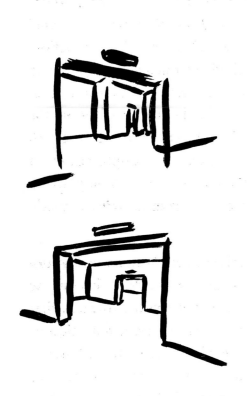

Taken together, Opie's works since 1986 mark a qualitative change in how things are disclosed to us. According to the traditional phenomenological account, things appear within a horizon (for which the 'world' is another name), including spatio-temporal location, symbolic and interpretative expectations, habits and customs. Phenomenology is, then, an investigation of the constitution of horizons. As a reflective approach this involves the projection of a horizon or horizons, or a 'beyond' – being, time, the infinite – as the condition of possibility for determinate horizons. It is not difficult to see how the project of phenomenology overlaps with that of aesthetic Modernism, which involves a series of concrete reflections on modes of disclosure. The question which needs to be asked, though, concerns the horizon or condition of possibility of the modernist reflection itself: to what extent does Modernism depend on a utopian or redemptive horizon of expectation? And what would be the result when accelerated modernisation meets with the loss of such a horizon?

With respect to this question Opie's work is profoundly ambivalent, and for the following reason. On the one hand, his whole oeuvre could be read as a mourning of Modernism, a pessimistic representation of the loss of a utopian horizon where Modernism is left just ticking over and little remains other than the narcissistic pleasures of irony and technological fetishism. On the other hand, Opie is able to continue the 'realist' side of the modernist project,[7] where modernisation and the experience of modernity are reflected not so much in representation as in modes of making and perception of the work, precisely because the loss of a utopian horizon has come to correspond with a new phenomenological experience of modernity. Thus, whilst art practice remains archaic with respect to current technological modes of production, image processing, etc., the phenomenological experience of

modernity has only just begun to catch up with what advanced art has known for a long time. The name for this experience, and this knowledge, is 'atopia'.

Atopia

Atopia means, literally, 'non-place'. A 'place' is somewhere that is symbolically marked, defined by limits or borders, constituted in relation to otherness (both within and without), and recognised through memory and tradition (whether actual or ideologically created). 'Place' is thus distinct from 'space' which is its abstraction: spatialisation involves the bracketing out of so-called 'secondary qualities' and symbolic-traditional residues for the sake of the derivation of location from co-ordinates on a grid. Constructivist Modernism could be said to involve the idealisation of pure spatiality coupled with a conception of freedom associated with the infinite (Opie's 'Bauhaus fish tanks' could be taken as a displacement of precisely this idealisation and this conception of freedom). Atopia as 'non-place' is not the same as constructivist pure space, even if it follows from it. Where exactly does the difference lie?

If the condition for the disclosure of pure space is the infinite horizon or horizon of the infinite, the horizon of atopia is not infinite but *indefinite*. Whereas the infinite necessarily implies a *telos,* a progression, even if asymptotic, towards that which recedes, the indefinite combines movement with inertia, and a reduction of identity and difference to the Same. Moreover, atopia is distinct from the infinity of pure space in that it is spatially located: as with 'place', one can enter and leave it. Thus it is not simply the negation of place, but a peculiar kind of 'positive' place with its own characteristics and temporality, and associated experiences. We are in a non-place when we cross passport control and enter the 'duty-free' area and pass on into the aeroplane; we are in a non-place when we sit in our cars, listening to the radio or a tape, driving along the motorway; we are in a non-place when we are at a shopping mall; we are in a non-place when we sit in the lobby of a corporate

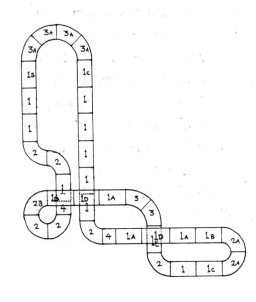

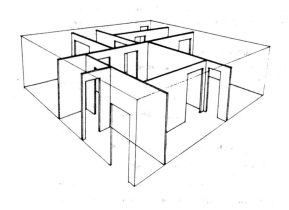

office waiting for an interview or a meeting. Perhaps one of the most typical of non-places is the computer games arcade. In each case, subjectivity does not disappear but is constituted through an impersonal mode of address: we are a passenger, a credit-card number, a score.[8] Non-places involve the displacement and destruction of places, since they are, unlike 'space', on the same level. This occurs where history is reconstituted as the 'historic': the use of the word 'experience' in such contexts – 'the X experience' – indicates an aestheticisation of history. Clearly non-places also involve their own peculiar – sometimes perverse – pleasures, not least that of doing something while doing nothing, of cutting free from the past with its ties and responsibilities, of enjoying the narcissistic pleasure of pure consumption.

Virtual reality is the apotheosis of atopia. In virtual reality, atopia, although still to be entered and left, is in principle freed even from the limits of 'natural' or Euclidean space. Narcissism is no longer dependent on the mirror-reflection, haunted by the Echo of Otherness. Freed from representation, narcissism becomes operative, susceptible to the pleasures of an indefinitely responsive non-world, pleasures just one step from the terror of psychosis, the loss of any symbolic constraint. Imagination, as Opie recognises in some of the titles of works of 1992–93 (*Imagine you are flying, Imagine you can order these, Imagine it's raining, Imagine you are driving*), has become a technology; or perhaps technology has become the Sublime, exceeding any human capacity to imagine or represent it, with virtual reality providing the 'safe' vantage point from which this monstrous excess may be apprehended.[9]

Is 'atopia' the truth of utopia itself, which in its double etymology refers both to 'happy place' and 'nowhere'?

But just as there exists no 'place' that cannot be appropriated by 'non-place', 'thematised' in a word, and no space outside theory which is pure, so there is no atopia which cannot be resymbolised, displaced and reappropriated in its turn. If the white-walled box of the modernist art gallery anticipates the phantasmic

seductions of atopia, so equally it becomes the site of its reconfiguration. Such reconfiguration generates meaning, I would suggest, by analogy, by a logic of relations rather than a (representational) logic of entities, just as the operative model of the artist replaces that which combines the artisan and the demiurge: Opie, precisely, acts in the space between the two. If, in a sense, this analogical constitution of meaning involves a return to the world of similitudes and correspondences which persisted from the mediaeval period into the Renaissance, it is without any ground in the order of being or a master-text to be read through the signatures left by God in Creation. The ultimate reference becomes nothing other than human finitude and corporeal existence. As Nietzsche taught us, the artist operates on a tight-rope over an abyss.

Notes:

1   *Le Virtuel. Vertus et vertiges*, Seyssel, Champvallon/ Institut National de l'Audiovisuel, 1993, p.85.

2   We may be the 'primitives' of a new order that has yet to be conceptualised. See Opie's statement in *Frieze*, issue 10, May 1993, p.33, where he compares computer imagery with early Renaissance painting: 'Although it is incredibly sophisticated, it also looks very primitive.' The issue is discussed in an accompanying article by James Roberts, 'Tunnel Vision', pp.27–35.

3   For a discussion of Opie's work in relation to perception, the body and Modernism, see my essay 'Undecidable Objects' in *Julian Opie*, exhibition catalogue, Lisson Gallery, London, 1988.

4   G-W Press, London, published by Liam Gillick and Jack Wendler.

5   For Aristotle, *techne* is art more or less in the sense of skill or craft, a deliberative virtue or knowledge which is of low level by comparison with theoretical knowledge, but nonetheless a way of disclosing or revealing truth, linked with *poiesis* as the activity of producing which sets to work what *techne* reveals. It is deficient according to Aristotle because its end lies in a product outside the agent. Thus even in its early usage *techne* embodies a tension between the disclosure of truth – or truth *as* disclosure – and an instrumental relation to the world. Today to an ever greater extent the world is disclosed just as technologically produced or artefactual, the result of technology but not necessarily as intended by any agent. Through a displacement from function to 'disinterested' perception, art may expose the artefactual nature of the world, but at the risk of coinciding with new, spectacular forms of consumerism which involve precisely a forgetting of the kinds of knowledge or memory intimated in art.

6   See James Roberts, *Julian Opie*, exhibition catalogue, Kunsthalle Berne/ Wiener Secession, 1991/92, §1, and Ulrich Loock's essay 'A Secret without a Secret' in the same catalogue.

7   See *Art in Theory: 1900–1990*, Charles Harrison and Paul Wood ed., Oxford, 1992, pp.128–129.

8   For a discussion of 'non-places', see Marc Augé, *Non-Lieux. Introduction à une anthropologie de la surmodernité*, Paris, 1992.

9   A lecture by Prof. Bob Spence of Imperial College, London titled 'Imagine that! The manner in which humans and computers will interact in the future is limited mainly by our imagination' was delivered at the Annual Festival of the British Association for the Advancement of Science, Keele University, 1st September 1993.

88

Imagine you can order these (2)
1992, acrylic on wood, glass and
aluminium
160 × 160 × 7 cm

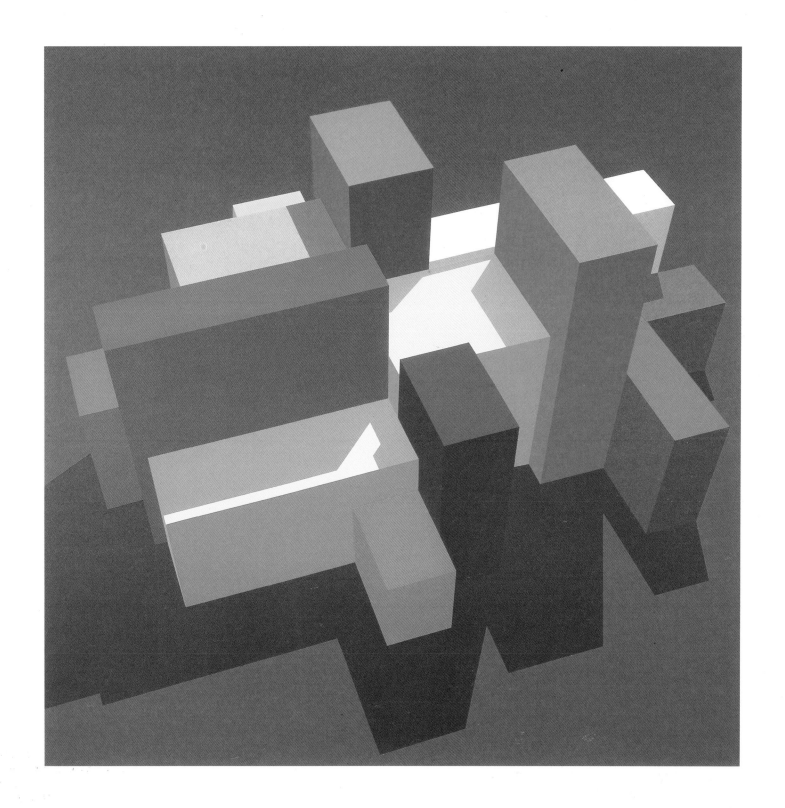

Imagine you can order these (3)
1992, acrylic on wood, glass and
aluminium
77 × 92 × 6 cm

Imagine you can order these (4)
1992, acrylic on wood, glass and
aluminium
77 × 92 × 6 cm

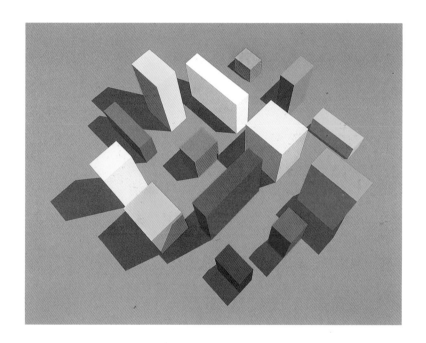

Imagine you can order these (5)
1992, acrylic on wood, glass and
aluminium
97 × 128 × 6 cm

Imagine you can order these (6)
1992, acrylic on wood, glass and
aluminium
97 × 128 × 6 cm

Overleaf: Imagine you can order these
(Sculpture 1, 2 & 3 of 7, layouts 2, 1, 3),
1993, oil paint on concrete
12 parts each

Overleaf: Imagine you can order these
(Sculpture 1, 2 & 3 of 7, layouts 2, 1, 3),
1993, oil paint on concrete
12 parts each

96

Imagine you are walking (1–18)
1993, acrylic on wood
25 × 33 cm each

Overleaf, left to right:
Imagine you are walking (Wall Painting 1 & 2)
1993, emulsion paint; dimensions variable

Imagine it's raining
1992, gloss paint on plywood
27 units in 3 groups:
group 1: 55 × 48 × 14 cm,
group 2: 161 × 144 × 40 cm,
group 3: 500 × 430 × 122 cm

Farmhouse
1993, painted plywood
175 × 120 × 230 cm

Fortified Farm
1993, painted plywood
140 × 200 × 230 cm

Castle
1993, painted plywood
250 × 100 × 135 cm

Country Church
1993, painted plywood
114 × 131 × 47 cm

Imagine you are driving (9 & 10)
1993, acrylic on wood, glass and
aluminium
93 × 123 × 3 cm

Imagine you are driving (11 & 12)
1993, acrylic on wood, glass and
aluminium
93 × 123 × 3 cm

Imagine you are driving (7)
1993, acrylic on wood, glass and
aluminium
93 × 123 × 3 cm

Imagine you are driving (8)
1993, acrylic on wood, glass and
aluminium
93 × 123 × 3 cm

Overleaf: **Fortified Area**
1993, concrete
27 parts 24 × 14 × 44 cm each
17 parts 36 × 15 × 15 cm each
Installation, Venice Biennale, 1993

Imagine you are driving
(sculptures 3 and 1),
1993, concrete

Overleaf:
Imagine you are driving (sculpture 2),
1993, concrete

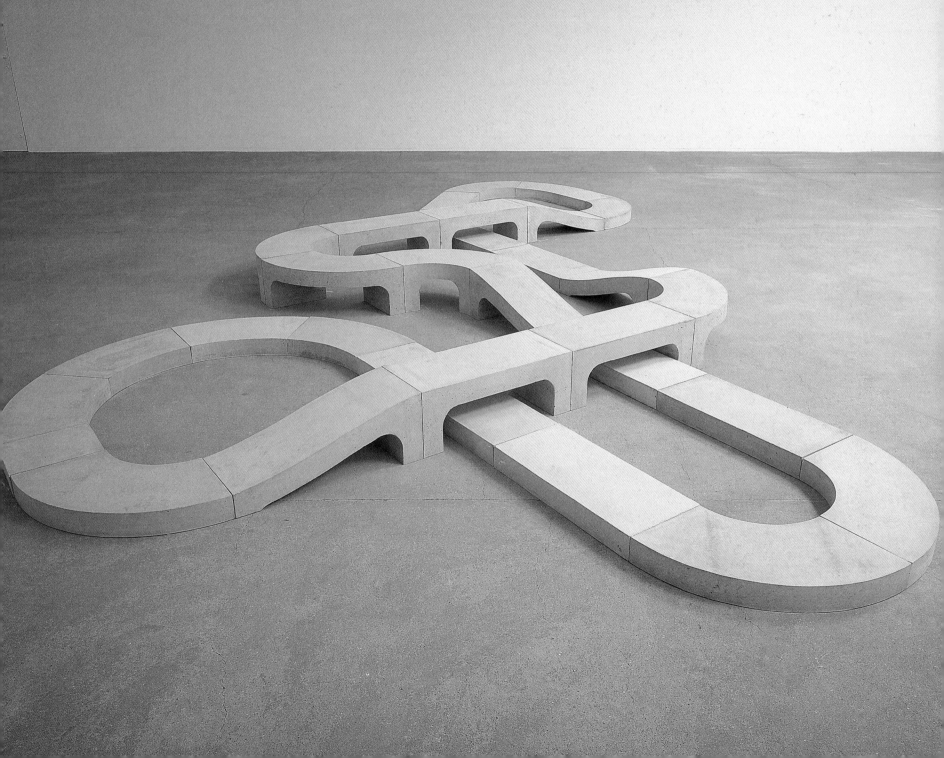

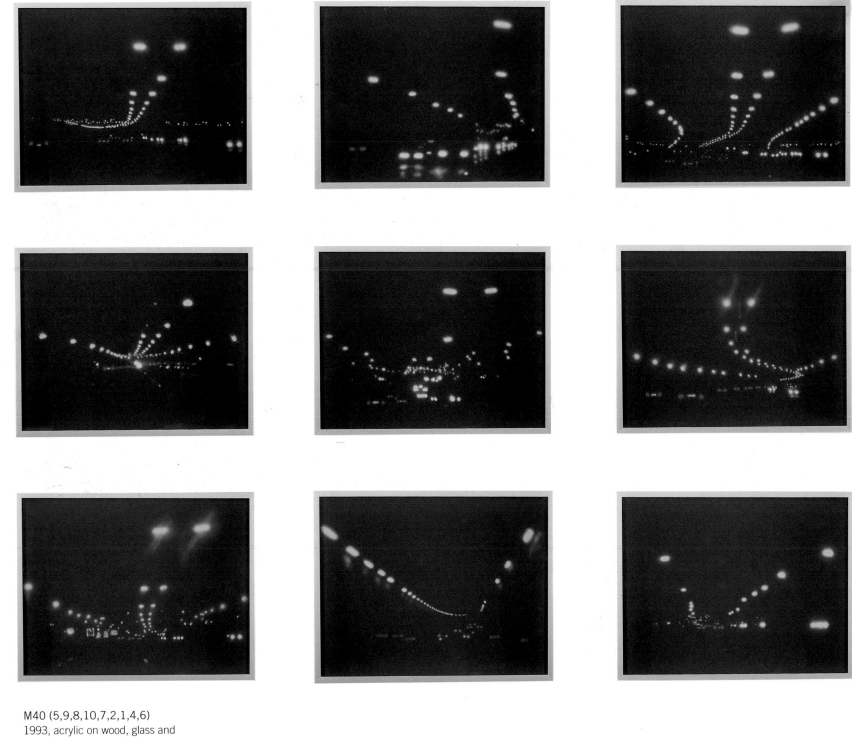

M40 (5,9,8,10,7,2,1,4,6)
1993, acrylic on wood, glass and
aluminium
32 × 42 cm each

M40 (3)
1993, acrylic on wood, glass and
aluminium
32 × 42 cm

M40 (2)
1993, acrylic on wood, glass and
aluminium
32 × 42 cm

M40 (4)
1993, acrylic on wood, glass and
aluminium
32 × 42 cm

Julian Opie

1958
Born in London

1979–82
Goldsmiths' School of Art, London

One-person exhibitions

1983
Lisson Gallery, London

1984–85
Kölnischer Kunstverein, Cologne (travelled to Groninger Museum, Groningen, Holland)

1985
Lisson Gallery, London
Institute of Contemporary Arts, London

1986
Franco Toselli Gallery, Milan
Lisson Gallery, London

1988
Lisson Gallery, London
Galeria Montenegro, Madrid
Galerie Paul Maenz, Cologne

1990–91
Lisson Gallery, London

1991
Kohji Ogura Gallery, Nagoya, Japan (with the support of
The British Council)
Galerie Luis Campaña, Frankfurt
Jänner Galerie, Vienna
Galleria Franz Paludetto, Turin
Primo Piano, Rome
Kunsthalle, Berne

1992
Wiener Secession, Vienna
Galerie Albrecht, Munich

1993
Hayward Gallery, The South Bank Centre, London

Group exhibitions

1982
Lisson Gallery, London
'Sculpture For a Garden', (Hounslow Sculpture II), Gunnersbury Park, London

1983
Charterhouse Square, London
'Young Blood', Riverside Studios, London
'Beelden/Sculpture 1983', Rotterdam Arts Council, Rotterdam
'The Sculpture Show', Hayward and Serpentine Galleries, London (organised by the Arts Council of Great Britain)
'8 Sculptors' Drawings', Air Gallery, London
'Making Sculpture', Tate Gallery, London

1984
'Artists for the 1990s – 10 Galleries, 10 Artists', Paton Gallery, London
'Underwater', Plymouth Arts Centre, Plymouth
Sculpture Symposium 1984, St Jean-Port, Quebec
'William Morris Today', Institute of Contemporary Arts, London
'Perspective '84', Internationale Kunstmesse, Basel
'Julian Opie and Lisa Milroy', Fondation Cartier pour l'art contemporain, Jouy-en-Josas, France
'Metaphor and/or Symbol: A Perspective on Contemporary Art', The National Museum of Modern Art, Tokyo (travelled to the National Museum of Art, Osaka)

1985
'The British Show' (organised by The Art Gallery of New South Wales, Sydney and The British Council) (and tour)
'XIIIème Biennale de Paris', Grande Halle de la Villette, Paris
'Still Life: A New Life', Harris Museum and Art Gallery, Preston (and tour)
'Anniottanta' (organised by La Cultura del Commune di Ravenna) (and tour)
'Three British Sculptors: Richard Deacon, Julian Opie and Richard Wentworth', The Israel Museum, Jerusalem

'Place Saint Lambert Investigations', Espace Nord, Liège
'Figure 1', Aberystwyth Arts Centre, Wales
'Sculpture in a Garden', Bluecoat Gallery, Liverpool

1986
'Forty Years of Modern Art 1945–1985', Tate Gallery, London
'Skulptur – 9 Kunstnere fra Storbrittanien', Louisiana Museum of Modern Art, Humlebaek, Denmark
'XVII Triennale di Milano', Milan
'De Sculptura – Eine Ausstellung der Wiener Festwochen 1986', Wiener Festwochen im Messepalast, Vienna
'Englische Bildhauer', Galerie Harald Behm, Hamburg
'Prospect 86. Eine internationale Austellung aktueller Kunst', Frankfurter Kunstverein, Frankfurt
'Correspondentie Europa', Stedelijk Museum, Amsterdam
'Focus on the Image: Selection from the Rivendell Collection' (organised by the Art Museum Association of America) (and tour)

1987
'Terrae Motus', Grand Palais, Paris (organised by Fondazione Amelio, Naples)
'British Art of the 1980s: 1987', Liljevalchs Konsthall, Stockholm (organised by The British Council) (and tour)
'Casting an Eye', Cornerhouse, Manchester

1988
'Europa oggi/Europe now', Museo d'Arte Contemporanea, Prato, Italy
'Les Années 80: A la Surface de la Peinture', Centre d'Art Contemporain, Abbaye Saint-André; Meymac Wolff Gallery, New York
'Britannica: 30 Ans de Sculpture', Musée des Beaux Arts André Malraux, Le Havre (and tour)
'British Sculpture 1960–1988', Museum van Hedendaagse Kunst, Antwerp

1989
'Grenville Davey, Michael Craig-Martin, Julian Opie', Lia Rumma Gallery, Naples
'Mediated Knot', Robbin Lockett Gallery, Chicago
'Object/Objectif', Galerie Daniel Templon, Paris
'Skulptur Teil II', Galerie Six Friedrich, Munich
'D+S Austellung', Hamburg Kunstverein, Hamburg
'Filling in the Gap', Feigen Gallery, Chicago

1990
'OBJECTives: The New Sculpture', Newport Harbor Art Museum, Newport Beach, California
'The British Art Show 1990' (organised by The South Bank Centre), McLellan Galleries, Glasgow; Leeds City Art Gallery; Hayward Gallery, London
'Biennale of Sydney', Sydney
'Studies on Paper: Contemporary British Sculptors', Connaught Brown, London
'Bild und Wirklichkeit', Galerie Albrecht, Munich
'Sculpture', Margo Leavin Gallery, Los Angeles
'Real Allegories', Lisson Gallery, London
'Work in progress: International Art in the Caja de Pensiones Foundation Collection', Caja de Pensiones Foundation, Madrid

1991
'Kunst Europa', Kunstverein Pforzheim, Germany (organised by The British Council)
'Objects for the Ideal Home: The Legacy of Pop Art', Serpentine Gallery
'A View of London', Künstlerhaus, Salzburg; Galleria Locus Solus, Genoa
'Centenary Exhibition', Goldsmiths' Gallery, London
'Confrontaciones 91', Palacio Velazquez, Madrid

1992
'Like nothing else in Tennessee', Serpentine Gallery, London
'Whitechapel Open', Whitechapel Art Gallery, London
'New Voices, New Works for The British Council Collection', (organised by The British Council), Centre de Conférences Albert Borschette, Brussels (and tour)
'Julian Opie, Jürgen Albrecht, Tim Head, Yuriko Kurimoto', Foro per l'Arte Contemporanea, Verona
'Paolo Uccello: spazio e colore, tempo e materia, luce e forma, Battaglie dell'Arte nel XX secolo', La Salerniana, Erice; Sale del Bramante, Rome

1993
'In Site - New British Sculpture', Museet for Samtidskunst, Oslo
'Machines for Peace', ex-Yugoslavian Pavilion, Venice Biennale
'Juxtapositions', Charlottenborg, Copenhagen
'Made Strange', Ludwig Museum, Budapest; Padiglione dell' Arte Contemporanea, Milan

Selected Bibliography:
books and catalogues

1983
Making Sculpture, Tate Gallery, London (catalogue)
The Sculpture Show, The Arts Council of Great Britain, London (catalogue),
text by Fenella Crichton
Beelden 83, Rotterdam Arts Council, Rotterdam (catalogue), text by Paul Hefting

1984
Julian Opie, Kölnischer Kunstverein, Cologne (catalogue, texts by Wulf
Herzogenrath and Kenneth Baker
Metaphor and/or Symbol, A Perspective on Contemporary Art, The National
Museum of Modern Art, Tokyo (catalogue), text by Masanori Ichikawa

1985
Julian Opie, Lisson Gallery, London (catalogue), texts by Michael Craig-Martin
and Art & Language
Drawings 1982 to 1985, Institute of Contemporary Arts, London (catalogue)
The British Show, Art Gallery of New South Wales, Sydney (catalogue), text by
Michael Newman
XIIIème Biennale de Paris, Biennale de Paris (catalogue)
Still Life: A New Life, Harris Museum and Art Gallery, Preston (catalogue)
Anniottanta, La Cultura del Commune di Ravenna, Ravenna (catalogue)
Three British Sculptors: Richard Deacon, Julian Opie and Richard Wentworth,
The Israel Museum, Jerusalem (catalogue)

1986
XVII Triennale di Milano, Milano (catalogue), text by Georges Teyssot
De Sculptura – Eine Ausstellung der Wiener Festwochen 1986, Wiener
Festwochen, Vienna (catalogue), text by Harald Szeemann
Correspondentie Europa, Stedelijk Museum, Amsterdam (catalogue)
Forty Years of Modern Art 1945–1985, Tate Gallery, London (catalogue)
Skulptur – 9 Kunstnere fra Storbrittanien, Louisiana Museum of Modern Art,
Humlebaek, Denmark (catalogue)
Prospect 86, Eine internationale Austellung aktueller Kunst, Frankfurter
Kunstverein, Frankfurt (catalogue)
Focus on the Image: Selection from the Rivendell Collection, The Art Museum
Association of America (catalogue)

1987
British Art of the 1980s, The British Council, London (catalogue)
Terrae Motus, Fondazione Amelio, Istituto per l'Arte Contemporanea, Naples
(catalogue)

Julian Opie, Documenta '87, Kassel (catalogue), text by Lynne Cooke
Britannia, Paintings and Sculptures from the 1980s, Sara Hilden Art Museum,
Tampere, Finland (catalogue)

1988
Europa oggi/Europe Now, Amnon Barzel ed., Museo d'Arte Contemporanea,
Prato (catalogue), text by Michael Newman
Julian Opie, Lisson Gallery, London (catalogue), text by Michael Newman
Les Années 80: A la Surface de la Peinture, Centre d'Art Contemporain, Abbaye
Saint-André, Meymac (catalogue), texts by Bernard Lamarche-Vadel and Gérard-
Georges Lemaire
Britannica: 30 Ans de Sculpture, Musée des Beaux Arts André Malraux, Le Havre;
Musée d'Evreux, Evreux; Ecole d'Architecture de Normandie, Rouen (catalogue),
texts by Catherine Grenier, Françoise Cohen and Lynne Cooke

1989
British Object Sculptors of the '80s II, Marco Livingstone ed., ArT Random,
Kyoto, Japan
Mediated Knot, Robbin Lockett Gallery, Chicago (catalogue), text by Kathryn
Hixson
Object/Objectif, Galerie Daniel Templon, Paris (catalogue), texts by David Moos
and Rainer Crone
D+S Austellung, Hamburg Kunstverein, Hamburg (catalogue)
New British Art in the Saatchi Collection, text by Alistair Hicks, London

1990
The British Art Show 1990, The South Bank Centre, London (catalogue), texts by
Caroline Collier, Andrew Nairne and David Ward
OBJECTives: The New Sculpture, Newport Harbor Art Museum, Newport
Beach, California (catalogue), text by Kenneth Baker
Biennale of Sydney, Sydney (catalogue)
Work in progress, International Art in the Caja de Pensiones Fundacion, Caja de
Pensiones Fundacion, Madrid (catalogue)

1991
Technique Anglaise, Andrew Renton and Liam Gillick (ed.), London
Objects for the Ideal Home, The Legacy of Pop Art, Serpentine Gallery, London
(catalogue)
A View of London, Künstlerhaus, Salzburg (catalogue)
Julian Opie, Kohji Ogura Gallery, Nagoya, Japan (catalogue), text by James
Roberts
Confrontaciones 91, Palacio Velazquez, Madrid (catalogue)
A281/14(E), Julian Opie and G-W Press, London
Il Limite Delle Cose, Nella Nuova Scultura Inglese, Studio Oggetto, Milano
(catalogue), text by Enrico Pedrini, Emilio Stabilini

1992
Julian Opie, Kunsthalle, Berne and Wiener Secession, Vienna (catalogue)
New Voices, New Works for The British Council Collection The British Council, (catalogue), text by Gill Hedley
Terrae Motus alla Reggia di Caserta, Fondazione Amelio, Istituto per l'Arte Contemporanea, Naples (catalogue)

1993
In Site/New British Sculpture, *Threshold*, No 9, January, Museet for Samtidskunst, Oslo (catalogue and magazine), texts by Karin Hellandsjø and Tim Marlow
Recent British Sculpture from the Arts Council Collection, The South Bank Centre, London (catalogue)
Juxtaposition, Sculpture, Charlottenborg, Copenhagen (catalogue)

Selected Bibliography: articles and reviews

1983
Marina Vaizey, 'Playing serious games', *The Sunday Times*, 24 April
John Russell Taylor, 'Young Blood', *The Times*, 26 April
Fiona Byrne-Sutton, 'Riverside Studio: Young Blood', *Art Line*, no. 7, June
Waldemar Januszczak, 'Three into two won't go', *The Guardian*, 16 August
William Feaver, 'From Camel to Camay', *The Observer*, 21 August
Mary Rose Beaumont, 'The Sculpture Show', *Arts Review*, September, pp. 474–475
Alistair Hicks, 'Talent under protection', *Mercury*, September, p. 36
William Feaver, 'Mr Futile's Progress', *The Observer*, 2 October
Sandra Miller, *Art Press*, no. 75, November
Jutta Koether, 'Julian Opie, Die Sympathische Plastik', *Spex Musik zur Zeit*, Cologne, no. 12, December, pp. 52–53
Michael Newman, 'The Bankable Sculpture of Julian Opie', *The Face*
Sarah Kent, 'Julian Opie', *Time Out*, 29 September

1984
Michael Newman, 'La Double Ironie de Julian Opie', *Art Press*, February, pp. 34–35
'Skulptur aus England', *Vorwärts*, Cologne, no. 8, August
Annelie Pohlen, 'Julian Opie und Tony Cragg', *Kunstforum*, no. 75, September-October, pp. 194–195
Ruud Schenk, 'Opie Verliefd', *Metropolis M*, no. 5, pp. 24–26

1985
Marina Vaizey, 'Having Fun with Trash', *The Sunday Times*, 13 April
William Packer, *The Financial Times*, London, 16 April
Sarah Kent, *Time Out*, London, 18 April
John Russell Taylor, 'A masterly turn to the South', *The Times*, 30 April
Waldemar Januszczak, 'The wage of affluence', *The Guardian*, 30 April
Richard Cork, 'In a Hurry', *The Listener*, 2 May
Mona Thomas, 'Intimes gentillesses du homme Julian Opie', *Beaux Arts Magazine*, no. 24, May, pp. 82–83
Richard Shone, 'London Exhibitions', *Burlington Magazine*, May
Christopher Andreae, 'Having a Fling with History', *Christian Science Monitor*, 29 June
Meir Ronnen, 'Life as a Pun', *Jerusalem Post Magazine*, Jerusalem, 16 August
'Design for London Living', *Avenue*, November, pp. 161–163
'Julian Opie, Ordinary Objects', *Metronom*, no. 4, p. 24

1986
Kenneth Baker, 'Julian Opie', *Louisiana Revy*, no. 2, March, pp. 23–37
Alistair Hicks, 'Breaking the mould', *The Magazine*, March, p. 43
Alistair Hicks, 'A rediscovery of power out of obscurity', *The Times*, November
'Sheets of Steel', *The Sunday Telegraph*, 9 November
'Julian Opie: Lisson Gallery', *Time Out*, 19 November
Larry Berryman, 'Julian Opie: Lisson Gallery', *Arts Review*, 5 December, p. 670

1987
Marina Vaizey, 'Life Studies', *Burlington Magazine*, January, pp. 45–49
Marjorie Allthorpe-Guyton, *Flash Art*, no. 132, February, p. 109
Stuart Morgan, 'Julian Opie: Lisson Gallery', *Artforum*, February, p. 131
Simon Watney, 'Julian Opie: Lisson', *Artscribe*, March, pp. 70–72
Lynne Cooke, 'Julian Opie and Simon Linke', *Flash Art*, no. 133, April, pp. 37–39
David Lovely, 'Casting an Eye: Cornerhouse', *Artscribe International*, May, p. 71
Diane B Paul, 'The Nine Lives of Discredited Data', *The Sciences*, May–June, pp. 26–30
Kenneth Baker, 'Julian Opie: Humorous, Cerebral Sculpture', *San Francisco Chronicle*, 13 June
Wolkenkratzer Art Journal, no. 4, p. 67
Paul Bonaventura, 'An Introduction to Recent British Sculpture', *Artefactum*, September–October, pp. 3–7

1988
Andrew Graham-Dixon, 'Pretty Vacant', *The Independent*, 8 March
Tom Baker 'House of Fun', *The Face*, April
'Exhibition Reviews', *Burlington Magazine*, April, p. 308
Kazu Kaido, *Bijutsu Techo*, Japan, vol. 40, no. 594, May, p. 16
Lynne Cooke, 'Identify the Object', *Art International*, vol. 3, summer, pp. 50–53
'Del caos al vacio del orden', *Guìa del Ocio*, Madrid, 17 October, p. 45

Jose Ramon Danvila, 'Julian Opie: el vacio atrapado', *El Punto*, Madrid, 21 October
Fernando Huici, 'Poérica de la indeterminación', *El Pais*, Madrid, 5 November
Norbert Messler, 'Julian Opie: Paul Maenz, Köln', *Noema*, November–December, p. 79
'Crónicas de exposiciones', *Lapiz*, no. 53, p. 83
Vicente Carreton Cano, 'La Oferta Inglesa', *Casa España Vogue*, no. 1
Rosa Olivares, 'Julian Opie', *Lapiz*, Spain, no. 52, p. 83

1989
'Julian Opie: Galeria Montenegro', *Arena*, February

1990
Edward Lucie-Smith, 'The British Art Show', *Modern Painters*, January
Liam Gillick, 'Critical Dementia: The British Art Show', *Art Monthly*, no. 134, March, pp. 14–16
John Russell Taylor, 'Taking a narrow view', *The Times*, 26 March
'Face Value', *The Standard*, London, 20 July
Catherine Lumby, 'Sydney Biennial, Art Gallery of New South Wales, Sydney', *Flash Art*, no. 153, summer, p. 180
Justin Hoffmann, 'Halley, Opie, Paolini, Albrecht', *Artscribe*, no. 83, September–October, pp. 93–94
Kenneth Baker, 'Physical Precision, notes on some recent sculpture', *Artspace*, September/October
Peter Frank, 'From the anti-form to the new Objecthood', *Artspace*, September–October, pp. 46–48
Rainer Metzger, 'Peter Halley, Julian Opie, Giulio Paolini: Susanne Albrecht', *Flash Art*, no. 154, October, pp. 162–163
James Carey Parkes, 'Julian Opie', *The Good Times*, 7 December
Louise Neri, 'Block's Buster: Eros, C'est la vie, The 8th Biennale of Sydney', *Parkett*, 25 September, pp. 143–148

1991
Sarah Kent, 'Julian Opie', *Time Out*, 2 January
Enrique Juncosa, 'Julian Opie', *Lapiz*, no. 75, February, pp. 88–89
Michael Archer, 'I was not making a monument, I was not making an object', *Art Monthly*, March, pp. 3–5
'Julian Opie: Lisson Gallery', *ARTnews*, vol. 90, no. 3, March
'From London', *BT Magazine*, March
Andrew Renton, 'Julian Opie, In between Space', *Flash Art*, no. 157, March–April, p. 134
Kiron Khosla, 'Julian Opie: Lisson Gallery', *Artscribe*, April
Steven Henry Madoff, 'Sculpture – A New Golden Age?', *ARTnews*, vol. 90, no. 5, May, pp. 110–121
Julia Cassim, 'Art transforms appliances', *The Japan Times*, Tokyo, 9 June, p. 11
Marco Livingstone, 'L'Heritage du pop art anglais leurres: voir double', *Art Press*, July–August, pp. 23–25

Rose Jennings, 'Eat your heart out, Andy', *New Statesman and Society*, September
Ralph Ubl, 'Die Macht der Tradition', *Die Presse*, 10 September
'Kunst: Nicht mehr und nicht weniger', *Kurier*, 27 September
'Julian Opie', *BT Magazine*, September
Charles Hall, 'The Legacy of Pop', *Arts Review*, 4 October
Konrad Tobler, 'Die Täuschung täuscht nur die Täuschung', *Berner Zeitung BZ*, 26 October
'Ushering in Banality', *RA magazine*, London, no. 32, autumn
Carolyn Christov-Bakargiev, 'Britannici tra i sette colli', *Domenica*, 17 November
Michael Archer, 'A View of London', *Das Jahr 91*, Salzburger Kunstverein
Gabrielle Boller, 'Grenville Davey/Julian Opie', *Das Kunst Bulletin*, no. 12, pp. 37–38
Nikkei Art 1991/92, p. 141
Floriana Piqué, 'Julian Opie: Franz Paludetto', *Flash Art*, December 1991

1992
Armando Testa, 'Ma le piante di Penone piaceranno ai Verdi?', *Il Giornale dell'Arte*, January, no. 96, p. 17
Enrique Juncosa, 'Julian Opie', *Lapiz*, February
Massimo Carboni, 'Julian Opie, Primo Piano', *Artforum*, Rome, February, p. 127
Fabrizio Crisafulli, *Juliet*, No. 56, February/March, p. 61
Georg Schöllhammer, 'Skulpturen der Trabantenstadt, Julian Opies Raum-modelle', *Der Standard*, Vienna, 26 February
Ulli Moser, 'Der Brite Julian Opie in der Wiener Secession', *Kurier*, Vienna, February
Gabrielle Boller, 'Grenville Davey, Julian Opie, Bern Kunsthalle', *Artefactum*, March, p. 49
'Julian Opie', *Vernissage*, Vienna, March
Kristian Sotriffer, 'Glätte und magie der Hülle: Julian Opie, Hübner und Zitko in der Secession', *Die Presse*, Vienna, March
Doris Krumpl, '1,800 elektronische Gewitter: die Secession zeigt neue Objekte des jungen Briten Julian Opie', *Falter*, Vienna
Günther Frohmann, 'Wien: Julian Opie, Ursula Hübner und Duane Hanson', *Salzburger Nachrichten*, Salzburg
Brigitte Borchhardt-Birbaumer, 'Wiener Secession: Opie, Hübner', *Wiener Zeitung*, Vienna
'Julian Opie in Wiener Secession', *Tiroler Tageszeitung*, Innsbruck, 16 March
Francesca Borrelli, 'Oriente mon amour', *Wimbledon*, no. 23, March, pp. 60–63
Clifford Myerson, 'Architectural Art', *Art Monthly*, London, May, pp. 22–24
Eva Karcher, 'Aktuell in Münchner Galerien', *Süddeutsche Zeitung*, Munich, 30 June
Charles-Arthur Boyer, 'De huizen van Julian Opie of: het vermoeide modernisme', *Archis*, September, p. 10

1993
James Roberts, 'Tunnel Vision', *Frieze*, issue 10, May, pp. 28–35

Works in Public Collections

Arts Council Collection, The South Bank Centre, London
Contemporary Art Society, Britain
Tate Gallery, London
Ludwig Forum für Internationale Kunst, Aachen
Israel Museum, Jerusalem
Stedelijk Museum, Amsterdam
Wadsworth Atheneum, Hartford, Connecticut
The British Council, London
Fundacion Caja de Pensiones, Madrid
Kunsthalle, Berne
Museo d'Arte Contemporanea, Prato
Deutsche Bank, Frankfurt
Calouste Gulbenkian Foundation, Lisbon
Lenbachhaus Städtische Galerie, Munich
Banque Bruxelles Lambert, Brussels
Museet for Samtidskunst, Oslo

Lenders to the exhibition

The British Council *Imagine you can order these No. 1.* 1992 (not in catalogue)
Collection Paul J. Leaman, Jr., New Orleans *Projekt for Heathrow*, 1985 (p. 16)
Agostino and Patrizia Re Rebaudengo, Turin *In order to cut glass it is necessary to score a line one molecule deep*, 1991 (p. 58)
Saatchi Collection, London *Soviet Frost (White II)*, 1986 (not in catalogue);
G., 1987 (p. 26); *J.*, 1987 (p. 26); *Night Light 18/3343BY*, 1989 (not in catalogue)
Suzanne & Selman Selvi Collection, Geneva *A Pile of Old Masters*, 1983 (p. 12)
Stedelijk Museum, Amsterdam *Divided They Stand, Divided They Fall*, 1986 (p. 20)
Tate Gallery, London *H.*, 1987 (p. 25)
Mr and Mrs Vogliotti, Turin *Painting of Unbuilt Sculpture*, 1992 (not in catalogue)
Jack and Nell Wendler, London *M.*, 1988 (p. 25)
Private collection *Cruise (multi coloured IV)*, 1986 (p. 21)

All other works are courtesy of the Lisson Gallery, London

In addition to those works lent for the exhibition, the following works in private and public collections are reproduced in the catalogue:

Incident in the Library II, 1983, Collection Nicholas and Caroline Logsdail, London (p. 14)
A to B, 1984, Le Witt Collection, Chester, Connecticut (p. 14)
This One Took Ages to Make, 1983, Collection Mr and Mrs Alan Safir, New York (p. 15)
Legend of Europa, 1984, Private collection, New York (p. 15)
Spies (Red II), 1986, Collection Richard Deacon, London (p. 18)
Ceasefire (Black III), 1986, Saatchi Collection, London (p. 19)
Man Accused of Murder, 1986, Saatchi Collection, London (p. 20)
Postal Staff Return to Work, 1986, Museo Pecci, Prato (p. 21)
Night Light (12/3343BB), 1989, Arts Council Collection, The South Bank Centre, London (p. 30)
Night Light (19/1343GY), 1989, Collection Pino Casagrande, Rome (p. 30)
Night Light (24/1343BY), 1989, Collection Leslie Simon & Michael Kritchman, San Diego (pp. 30 and 31)
Night Light (25/333CB), 1989, Collection Leslie Simon & Michael Kritchman, San Diego (pp. 30)
Painting of D/889/E, 1991, Private collection (p. 55)
HA/45-11, 1990, Kunsthalle, Berne (p. 56)
Painting of It is believed that some dinosaurs could run faster than a cheetah, 1991, Private collection, London (p. 60)
There are 1800 electrical storms in the earth's atmosphere at any one time, 1991, Lenbachhaus Städliche Galerie, Munich (p. 63)
Imagine it's raining, 1991, Museet for Samtidskunst, Oslo (p. 100)

Photo credits: Sue Ormerod, Studio Blu, Turin, John Riddy, Stephen White, Gareth Winters